*Transforming Suffering*

*Edited by Donald W. Mitchell*

*and James Wiseman, O.S.B.*

**DOUBLEDAY**

NEW YORK   LONDON   TORONTO   SYDNEY   AUCKLAND

# Transforming Suffering

REFLECTIONS ON FINDING PEACE

IN TROUBLED TIMES

BY HIS HOLINESS THE DALAI LAMA,

HIS HOLINESS POPE JOHN PAUL II,

THOMAS KEATING,

THUBTEN CHODRON,

JOSEPH GOLDSTEIN,

AND OTHERS

PUBLISHED BY DOUBLEDAY

a division of Random House, Inc.

DOUBLEDAY and the portrayal of an anchor with a dolphin are registered trademarks of Random House, Inc.

Library of Congress Cataloging-in-Publication Data

Transforming suffering: reflections on finding peace in troubled times / by His Holiness the Dalai Lama . . . [et al.]; edited by Donald W. Mitchell and James Wiseman.—1st ed.

p. cm.

Includes index.

1. Suffering—Religious aspects—Catholic Church—Congresses.
2. Suffering—Religious aspects—Buddhism—Congresses. I. Bstan-'dzin-rgya-mtsho, Dalai Lama XIV, 1935–   II. Mitchell, Donald W. (Donald William), 1943–  III. Wiseman, James A., 1942–

BT732.7 T73 2003

291.2'2—dc21

2002041323

ISBN 0-385-50782-8

*Book design by Lisa Sloane*

PRINTED IN THE UNITED STATES OF AMERICA

September 2003

First Edition

1 3 5 7 9 10 8 6 4 2

# Contents

# Preface

At a relaxed weekend retreat in mid-May of 1999, a small group of American Buddhist leaders met with representatives of Monastic Interreligious Dialogue, or MID for short, at the retreat center of the Insight Meditation Society in Barre, Massachusetts. The Buddhist leaders included a Zen master from the West Coast, a Tibetan *geshe* representing His Holiness the Dalai Lama, and the host of the retreat from the Insight Meditation Society. The MID representatives included two Benedictine monastics, a Trappist monk, and an MID lay advisor. This meeting in the gentle, wooded hills of Massachusetts was the result of a long journey of dialogue spanning decades of encounters throughout Asia, Europe, and North America.

In 1968, Benedictine abbots sponsored the first Asian East-West Intermonastic Conference in Bangkok, Thailand, dedicated to the encounter of Western monastic spirituality with Eastern spiritual traditions. This was the conference that brought Thomas Merton to Asia and to visit His Holiness the Dalai Lama. Merton and His Holiness instantly became "spiritual brothers," and a connection was forged between Tibetan Buddhism and Christian monasticism. Tragically, Merton died while attending the Bangkok conference. Some have said that his untimely death produced a seed for spiritual encounter between East and West.

In 1974, the Benedictine Confederation was asked by the Vatican to pursue the creation of an interfaith "bridge and contact point" in the monastic world for promoting mutual understanding concerning the spiritual life. The leadership of the confederation responded to this invitation by encouraging the founding of two organizations. In North America, what would become known as Monastic Interreligious Dialogue (MID) was formed in 1977. A few months later in Europe, Dialogue Interreligieux Monastique (DIM) was founded.

The aim of these two organizations is to foster interreligious dialogue, exchanges, and collaboration, especially between Buddhist and Christian monastics. With the support of MID and DIM, during the 1980s and 1990s numerous Buddhist monks and nuns traveled to Christian monasteries and convents from the desert of New Mexico to the mountain top of Montserrat, Spain. Meanwhile, Christian monks and nuns visited ancient Buddhist monasteries from the peaceful center of Kyoto to the remote areas of Tibet.

In all of these encounters, a spiritual dialogue from the hearts and minds of masters in the spiritual life took place as hosts and visitors developed a deeper trust and respect for each other's traditions. As spiritual friendships were forged, more practical issues were also addressed. MID began, for example, to help its Tibetan brother monks and sister nuns gain healthcare expertise, computer skills, and education needed to better serve their people living in exile in India.

A turning point in this journey of spiritual dialogue took place in 1993, when His Holiness was attending MID's intermonastic dialogue at the Parliament of the World's Religions in Chicago. After the program, His Holiness told members of MID that he felt the ground had been sufficiently prepared for an in-depth, worldwide encounter between spiritual leaders from Buddhism and Christianity. His Holiness suggested that twenty-five Buddhist and twenty-five Christian spiritual teachers be invited to live, pray, meditate, and dialogue together about spirituality and its importance for the modern world. He asked if it would be possible to hold this historic, global East-West encounter at the Abbey of Gethsemani, home of his dear friend Thomas Merton.

Following the suggestions of His Holiness the Dalai Lama, MID hosted in July 1996 what is now referred to as the famous Gethsemani Encounter. At this historic event in the rolling hills of Kentucky, His Holiness was joined by Buddhist spiritual teachers from India, Sri Lanka, Thailand, Myanmar, Cambodia, Taiwan, Korea, Japan, and throughout Europe and North America. Christian teachers of spirituality came from Asia, Australia, Europe, and North America, including the

Abbot General of the Trappists from Rome, and representatives from the Vatican, the Benedictine Confederation in Rome, and the United States Conference of Catholic Bishops. The participants of the encounter lived together in the Abbey of Gethsemani, meditated together each morning, and attended each other's rituals.

The dialogue itself focused on aspects of spirituality in Buddhism and Christianity: the practice of prayer and meditation, the stages of growth in the spiritual life, the role of the spiritual teacher and the community, and the goals of spiritual and social transformation. Besides the fifty participants, over one hundred observers attended the Gethsemani Encounter. The dialogue was covered by National Public Radio, and a beautiful segment about it was aired during the Public Broadcasting Corporation's evening news.

To share the fruits of this incredible spiritual feast, MID published a book containing all of the talks by Christian and Buddhist spiritual teachers as well as some of the actual dialogue. The book is entitled *The Gethsemani Encounter: A Dialogue on the Spiritual Life by Buddhist and Christian Monastics,* edited by Donald W. Mitchell and James Wiseman, O.S.B. (New York: Continuum, 1997). This book was chosen for the Book-of-the-Month Club, received the 2002 Frederick J. Streng Book Award, and was even touted on *Sports Center* by Phil Jackson.

Nearly three years after the Gethsemani Encounter, a small group of Buddhists and Christians who had participated in the event gathered for a weekend retreat in Barre, to ponder what the next step in this journey of spiritual dialogue might be. They remembered the sad and moving story told at Gethsemani of how a monastery of Trappist monks in North Africa had chosen to remain with their Muslim neighbors to provide them with support in facing the threat of terrorism that was plaguing the region. Unfortunately, seven of the brothers in that monastery were killed just a few months before the Gethsemani Encounter. The story was one of self-sacrificing love, of interfaith unity and solidarity, of being willing to give one's life for one's neighbor, and of forgiveness of one's enemies—even those who kill you. The members of the Barre group also remembered the Tibetan stories of oppression, torture, and exile, and the stories by Maha Ghosananda, the Supreme Buddhist Patriarch of Cambodia, concerning his ministry of peace and reconciliation to the Cambodian people during the time of the killing fields.

Concern for human suffering in today's troubled world surfaced again and again at the Gethsemani Encounter. The group at Barre felt strongly that "Yes, we *are* living in troubled times, and what can we do about it? What can our spiritual traditions offer to suffering humanity today?"

These questions reminded the Christian members of the group of Thomas Merton's challenge to monastic communities to make their walls thin enough to share their spiritual riches with the world, to share with those in need of guidance, support, and inspiration for daily living. In our hurried world, people with a few years of experience are offering advice to troubled hearts and minds. But the monastic traditions of Buddhism and Christianity have respectively 2,500 and 2,000 years of experience.

For millennia, monastic communities of men and women

around the world have sought together the secrets of peace and happiness. They have been successful in their search and have produced wisdom traditions East and West concerning the kinds of perennial problems that always trouble humankind: How do you find emotional healing? How do you deal with anger, or jealousy, or pride? How do you confront violence and abuse? How can you become free from unhealthy attachments to people and things, or status and security? How can you let go of control and find freedom? How do you accept sickness and aging . . . and eventually death? How, in the end, do you explain our suffering condition?

Buddhist and Christian monastics have sought answers to these and other questions about our human condition. The answers they have discovered deep in their hearts and minds, and in their relationships with each other, have led to truly humane and satisfying forms of living and loving, of compassion and peacefulness. These patterns of living have sustained men and women East and West for countless generations during wars, economic disasters, internal strife and scandal, social upheavals, plagues and poverty, oppression and terrorism. Through dark and painful times in human history, monasteries have remained over the centuries oases of wisdom, love, peace, and joy.

Given the many problems facing humankind at the beginning of this new millennium, this seems to be the time to share this wisdom with the world. So, the Barre group decided to request that another Gethsemani Encounter be held to address the ways we all suffer in troubled times. By "troubled times," we mean not only the social, economic, military, and political problems we are facing but also the emotional problems, the problems of aging and sickness, of the loss of loved ones, of facing our own mortality, and similar personal and relational problems. This is what the Barre group decided to suggest to His Holiness the Dalai Lama and to MID. They did, and plans began to be made to hold another Gethsemani Encounter to share with the world the spiritual advice and experience of both traditions on how to transform suffering for the healing of ourselves and our world.

In April 2002, the second Gethsemani Encounter was held to dialogue about ways of transforming suffering. This time the Buddhist and Christian participants who were invited were primarily persons who had years of training and experience in spiritual direction and guidance in the West. We began with talks and dialogue about the nature and meaning of suffering and how it can be transformed through spirituality. We then addressed particular forms of suffering that are most troubling today.

First, we dialogued about the ways people suffer from a sense of unworthiness and alienation, and the need for emotional healing. Second, we explored the ways that people today get caught in the web of consumerism and the need to find freedom in lives of compassion and caring for others. Third, we discussed how anger, hatred, and arrogance lead to both personal and institutional violence, and the need to overcome these unhealthy states of mind. Finally, we talked about how we have faced and dealt with the inevitable suffering that comes with aging, sickness, and death.

In all the talks and dialogues, our intent was to provide spiritual guidance, inspiration, and support to those who endure these and other forms of suffering. We not only wanted to *inform* people about suffering but also to help people in our troubled world *transform* their suffering. While the reflections on these topics speak for themselves, we want to add two clarifications.

First, while His Holiness the Dalai Lama helped organize this encounter and was planning to participate, he experienced health problems just prior to the date of the encounter and had to cancel all his travels for two months. However, His Holiness sent us his personal reflections on the transformation of suffering that, along with his prayers for the encounter, contributed greatly to the dialogue. Many of the Buddhist participants shared their reflections about the words of His Holiness in ways that were enriching and that showed even more clearly their value for humankind today. Also, Robert Aitken Roshi could not be at the dialogue because of health reasons; however, we have included his prepared remarks.

Second, each of the participants received a copy of His Holiness Pope John Paul II's apostolic letter, "On the Christian Meaning of Human Suffering" *(Salvifici Doloris)*. As his words played a valuable role in the conversations of the Gethsemani Encounter, we have placed a condensed version of his letter in this book. The dialogue that evolved about the Christian meaning of suffering led to a profound sharing of insights about the wisdom of the Cross, the abandonment of Christ, and deliverance/liberation by both Christians and Buddhists.

In editing the talks and transcripts of the dialogues, we placed those reflections that give us a Buddhist understanding of suffering and its transformation in Chapters 1 and 2. The reflections that present the Christian understanding of the nature and meaning of suffering and its transformation appear in Chapters 3 and 4. The reflections by Buddhists and Christians about abandonment, that of Jesus and of one's own, and love were placed in Chapter 5. At this point, it became clear that there was agreement that certain patterns of thinking, feeling, choosing, and acting nurture positive humane qualities of living, which, in turn, generate peace and happiness within oneself and in one's relationships with others. Reflections on these qualities—including love and kindness, compassion and care for those in need, and communion and unity in relationships—are included in Chapter 6.

These positive, healthy patterns and qualities of living are certainly compromised by the kinds of suffering conditions we discussed in the dialogue. Love and kindliness for oneself and others are sorely affected by a sense of worthlessness and alienation from others. Compassion and care for others are lessened by the isolation of self-centeredness and a consumer identity and orientation toward the world. Unity and communion are broken by thoughts and feelings of anger and hatred as well as abusive and violent words and deeds. These forms of suffering and their transformation are the focus of the reflections in Chapters 7 through 9.

Finally, there are some forms of suffering we all experience, no matter what the spiritual or ethical quality of our lives may be: sickness, aging, and facing our eventual death. These aspects of our human condition and their transformation are addressed by the reflections in Chapters 10 and 11. We conclude the book, in light of the events of September 11 and the theory of the clash of civilizations, with a short chapter of reflections on the need today for building a culture of dialogue and peace. A brief Epilogue shows the importance of this task.

It is our hope that this book will be a healing source of guidance and strength for many people who are on a personal journey to fuller peace and happiness and want to work with others to build a more peaceful and united humankind.

DONALD W. MITCHELL
*Purdue University*
JAMES WISEMAN, O.S.B.
*The Catholic University of America*

# CHAPTER ONE

# The Buddhist Understanding of Suffering

*Geshe Lhundub Sopa*

At the beginning of the twenty-first century, it seems that people around the world are deeply troubled. There are financial worries for some; poverty, hunger, and starvation for others. Family concerns and personal stress grow as people work harder and longer hours to purchase consumer goods. Environmental and social problems are everywhere, and we are faced with war, violence, and terrorism. These are troubling times.

The Buddha spoke of what he called *dukkha*. This word is hard to translate. Some translate it as *suffering*, but a better translation is *dissatisfaction*. *Dukkha* is actually an ancient word that refers to what happens when a wheel rubs because the hub is not on correctly. So, as our life goes along, we feel the rub, we experience dissatisfaction with how things are going. Religion cannot inoculate us against the painful conditions of life. We all get sick, lose loved ones, grow old, and eventually pass away. But religion can provide spiritualities that address *dukkha,* our dissatisfied mind or troubled heart in the midst of the painful conditions that life brings us. Spiritual practice can lead us to an inner peace expressed in loving kindness, compassion, and empathetic joy. Even in the midst of the troubles of life, we can find happiness.

This inner peace of mind and heart is important for many reasons. The Buddha points out that it is especially important due to the fact that our dissatisfied mind, our troubled heart, can lead us to think, feel, and act in ways that contribute to suffering, to making our troubling situations even more painful for ourselves and others. For example, our dissatisfaction with another person can lead to anger and even hatred for that person. Those feelings are troubling in themselves but can also lead to acts of violence. We also may be dissatisfied with other races, nations, or religions; and we may respond to this dissatisfaction as a group in ways that are hurtful.

The Buddha teaches that our dissatisfaction with others is connected to a belief that someone, some race or nation or religion, is separate and different from ourselves. Their differences are seen as threatening to us, to our satisfaction or happiness. So we define the other as an enemy. This, in turn, leads to all sorts of troubles. Here we find a fundamental ignorance of our common humanity, of the fundamental unity of life, of its interconnectedness of which we are all parts. It is this ignorance that we have to overcome in order to find inner peace and happiness in a way that also supports the peace and happiness of others.

### Venerable Henepola Gunaratana

I am the teacher in a meditation center. Normally, meditation centers draw people with troubles, especially younger people. Working with troubled people is a yeoman's task. We need to listen to them patiently and teach them by our example how to be patient with themselves. Patience does not mean that you let others walk all over you. It means waiting for the right time to say the right words with the right attitude to the right people.

We also need sometimes to agree with them and sometimes to agree to disagree with them. We never expect them to agree with what we tell them. If they don't agree with us, they need to feel free to say that they don't agree with us. And we both have to learn to agree to disagree. This is true not only for individuals but for societies, organizations, and religions. Everyone needs to learn to respect each other's cherished values, beliefs, and feelings. The ideal for the human family is harmony, unity with diversity.

*we address suffering*
*by scaling down slowing*
*down & listening*

### Reverend Heng Sure

I once took part in a church activity called Data Sabbath. People set aside their technological devices, taking a total break from the "power grid," and coming back to friends and family. For those of us who are troubled by the fast pace of modern life, this idea has much to offer. It shows us that real peace and happiness that are truly meaningful and satisfying are not to be found on a technological highway going a hundred miles an hour, but with no one at the wheel. When is there time to ask the big questions about where we are going? What is this life about? To take some time to slow down, to set the technological world aside and return to the divine, to nature, to family, to oneself is very important not only spiritually but humanly as well.

### Ajahn Sundara

Most people think that contemplative Buddhist monasteries are quiet and peaceful places and that we just sit on our cushions all day. Actually, monasteries can be filled with activities, and sometimes my life has never felt so busy! Yet there is a spaciousness in that kind of environment that allows all that we find difficult to experience and be with—our inner resistances, aversion, despair, a sense of the meaninglessness of it all—to be accepted in consciousness and let go of. Spaciousness on the physical, psychological, and spiritual levels allows the heart to rest and provide the context we need to allow change and healing to take place. Unfortunately, in our modern world, this commodity is considered pretty worthless. Thus, we rarely find the means to access that inner spaciousness of awareness so much needed to discover our own humanness and the way to real happiness.

*This invokes emptying which cani't be done without silence and slowness.*

### Venerable Chuen Phangcham

What does happiness mean? Some say that it means life without problems, having food, clothes, medicine, housing, and so on. For the Buddha, happiness is peacefulness, living peacefully without hatred, greed, anger, in the midst of the problematic situations of life. It means living with a calm and clear mind, an awakened mind that is free from delusion. The Buddha's path leads us to this Nirvana. *Honesty to self.*

The first level of the path has to do with changing how we live. We refrain from killing, stealing, lying, taking intoxicating drinks or harmful drugs, and any sexual misconduct. We cultivate a life of loving kindness, universal compassion, generosity, sincerity, truthfulness, mindfulness, and wisdom. Here are the seeds of true happiness.

On the second level of the path, we practice meditation to deepen these virtues in our mind and root out the vices that restrict our freedom. We develop a calm and peaceful mind, step by step. Mental defilements, unwholesome thoughts and feelings, are loosened and subdued; the mind becomes more and more free, loving, and wise.

On the third and final level of the path, we deepen our wisdom. We find that we are not separate from one another. We are one with others and part of the unity of all things. Everyone is a brother or sister to be loved. As this new vision of life grows in our consciousness, we feel united in heart with all beings and want to bring peace and harmony into the lives of everyone. In doing so, we not only find happiness, we bring it to everyone we meet. This is the ideal of the Buddha: "May peace prevail on earth, and may all living beings be happy."

### Venerable Henepola Gunaratana

There are many kinds of rings: wedding rings, engagement rings, earrings. But there is one ring that we all have, whether Buddhist, Hindu, Muslim, Christian, Jew, or no religion. All living beings have suffer*ing.* Suffering is universal. We cannot totally eliminate it. Because of our modern technology, we have discovered various things to combat suffering, prolong our life a bit, overcome many sicknesses, eliminate some poverty, provide better sanitation, and so forth. But in spite of all these modern developments, suffering still exists. It has not totally been eliminated. It can never be fully eliminated from the world.

For instance, can we stop falling sick? Can we stop growing old? Can we stop sorrow, lamentation, pain, grief, and despair caused by separation from loved ones? There is also suffering associated with not getting what we want, or getting what we do not want. And when we do have what we want, we worry about losing it or protecting it. Then when we look around us, we witness crimes, wars, killings—all kind of things that we really don't want to see or hear. But we do not have the capacity to stop these painful things. Today people are especially prone to the suffering of stress, fear and anxiety, nervousness and depression, worry and anger, restlessness and a lack of self-worth. These states of mind come and go as we adjust to the different stages of our lives.

Nobody is born with a big smile; everybody is born with a big cry. Why do we cry? We cry not only because we are separated from our mother's comfortable womb but because we are thrust into this world, and at that moment we start crying. This crying about our human condition continues all our life. It may not be always heard, but the cry is always going on deep within our hearts. That first cry is symbolic of the cry we carry for the rest of our life. The more beings there are, the more cries there are.

Now, being ignorant of the source of this cry in our hearts, we seek happiness in the things we enjoy in the world around us. We often think that something new can bring us happiness, like a new car or house. I once knew a man who had been married six times. He was certain that his next marriage would bring him the happiness he was seeking. But the truth is that no matter what we use to stop the crying, the suffering of our lives continues due to the fact that we do not understand it.

*The cry is always there*

Indeed, understanding suffering is essential in order to do something about it. Just as if we were sick and didn't know what was making us sick. Until we find out what kind of sickness we have, how can we find a cure?

Our inner cry has two causes. One is what we call in Buddhism an insatiable greed. By greed, we mean that there is something in us that is never satisfied. No matter what we have, we want more. The second is even more important. We call it ignorance. We don't know what it is that makes us so dissatisfied. There is something in us that does not understand what is happening that makes us dissatisfied or unhappy. These two causes combine and work together.

We Buddhists believe that our dissatisfaction, our unhappiness, our inner cry exists because of what we call clinging of attachment to self. It's like the word *onion*. How do you spell onion? O, N, with I in the middle, and then O, N again: on and on, with I in the middle. So, too, our crying goes on and on because I is in the middle. So long as we are attached to this I, our unhappiness continues to go on and on. Because of my attachment, my clinging to my concept of myself, we continue to be troubled. This is ignorance. Once we recognize that this "self" that I conceive myself to be is a mere concept, that it is not something substantial as I think it is, we will find freedom from our troubled minds and hearts. Our unhappiness and our crying will cease.

For example, self-identity is very important in Western psychology, and we do everything to promote it. When I was a little boy, about six years old living in a very poor village in Sri Lanka, I sat down and drew a beautiful pumpkin with my fingers in the sand in front of our home. I began to admire this pumpkin because it was mine. I created it, and I was attached to it. While I was enjoying looking at it, my sister, who was about four years older than me, came by, stopped, and erased the picture that I had drawn in the sand. I got so furious that I wanted to attack her. I looked around and found a block of wood. I hardly could lift it, but I managed and chased after her. She ran into the house and through the kitchen, hoping to run out the kitchen door. Unfortunately for her, the kitchen door was locked. When she stopped, I took that block of wood and threw it at her. It hit her foot and her big toenail broke off. She was crying, weeping, making a big commotion. Until this day, my sister still has that scar on her big toe. I created all this trouble for my sister, myself, and everyone because of my ignorant attachment to something that did not really exist. It was just a made-up pumpkin. And I suffer even now when I think about it.

We all make up our sense of selfhood, our identity, but it is just a concept. Our attachment to this self-concept brings us much suffering. So, in order to minimize our suffering, we need to redirect our thoughts in a positive, wholesome direction that leads to true happiness. We can begin to do this by developing an honest understanding of our attachments to our nonexisting, imaginary concept of selfhood. This is the goal of many of our meditation practices. Then with an understanding of our false self, we can begin letting go of that self. In letting go of this attachment to self, with all the related worries about ourselves and our unhealthy reactions to the world around us, we can begin to minimize our unhappiness.

*letting go of thisself through giving/kindness/meditation loving*

This letting go is what we call generosity. Generosity does not mean just letting go of material things. Sharing things with others is one aspect of generosity. Real generosity means letting go of this attachment to self. This letting go of self is also called "selflessness." Understanding our attachment to self is not easy. So, to cultivate this generosity, this selflessness, we also practice what is called loving kindness, or what I prefer to call loving friendliness. The word for loving kindness is *metta,* which is derived from the word for friend, *mitta.*

Loving friendliness is to be directed toward ourselves and toward others. It is opposed to self-hatred and hatred of others. As we live loving friendliness with a number of people, we reduce the suffering of those people. This practice is called "boundless" because it transcends all religions, all cultures, all races, all traditions—all boundaries. Its practice helps us break down conceptual limitations on our love and care for ourselves and for others. Everything is transcended when we cultivate this thought of loving friendliness. In fact, I think that one of the hallmarks of high world religions is that they all teach loving all living beings, respecting their dignity in a very basic way.

When we live this kind of loving friendliness, our self-centeredness is reduced, our openness to others is increased, and we can begin to let go of ourselves, our ignorant attachments to self. What is happening here is that we grow in compassion from the thought of loving friendliness. Compassion motivates us to reduce the suffering of others and opposes the selfish motivation to live for ourselves. As we live loving friendliness and compassion, we find that our happiness increases, and so does the happiness of others. We can at last begin to see a way of transcending our troubles and making our life more satisfying and peaceful.

Friends, this is the purpose of life. We all want to be peaceful and happy. Nobody does anything to make his or her life more troubled, miserable, unhappy. We always do things to make ourselves happy. But are we happy yet? Why not? No matter what we do to make ourselves happy, until we do the right things, we will never be happy. What are the right things? Understanding how we are attached to ourselves. Cultivating a generous heart by letting go of ourselves. Cultivating the thoughts of loving friendliness and compassion for ourselves and for all living beings.

*Keys to happiness*

### Abbot John Daido Loori

In the Buddhist tradition, there are several ways of dealing with our dissatisfactory way of living, our troubled mind and heart, our suffering existence. Ultimately, we seek the extinguishing of suffering, which is Nirvana. But there is also the alleviation of suffering, and there is the transformation of suffering.

*is the end of suffering Nirvana*

The extinguishing of suffering is the goal of monastic training. People who enter our Zen monastery are seeking to resolve the grave questions of life and death: Who am I? What is life? What is death? What is truth? What is reality? To find the answers to these ultimate questions, our students move through successive stages of training. *Zazen,* or sitting meditation, is at the core of all of these stages, indeed at the core of everything that we do. Here a student is trying to develop a single-pointedness of mind in dealing with the thoughts and the feelings that come up. It is a very slow process that takes place over many years.

Because Zen is an ancestral lineage, its teachings are conveyed from teacher to student rather than through scripture or study. It is one-to-one, mind-to-mind transmission. In that personal transmission, we use *koan* study. In unraveling these *koans* each day, the teacher and student meet face to face during periods of *zazen.* In our lineage, there are 750 *koans,* or paradoxical sayings, questions, or stories, that a student needs to go through over a period of between fifteen to twenty years, or sometimes more. These *koans* are designed to short-circuit the whole intellectual process. They essentially frustrate linear sequential thought and open up another aspect of consciousness, which is direct, immediate, and intuitive. That's where religious experience takes place, where freedom is found.

Our practice is guided by ethical teachings, the precepts. These precepts are aspects of a process of spiritual and moral maturing that develops throughout all stages of Zen practice. Related to this process in our training are the liturgies that punctuate our entire day. They take place not only in the Buddha hall, but when we begin work practice, or before we take a meal, or even before using the bathroom. Each event of the day has a liturgy that precedes it and reminds us what this activity is really about.

These liturgies are not worship services. Buddha is not a God, and Buddhism is nontheistic. It is not atheistic. Buddhism does not say that there is no God. Nor is Buddhism agnostic. It does not say I don't know if there is a God or not. Buddhism just doesn't take up the question of whether there exists a God, which keeps that whole question open in a very interesting way.

In the process of Zen monastic practice, there is certainly spiritual development. Through this development, some people may get to that place where suffering is extinguished, and some may not. But in any event, a spiritual maturity does indeed happen; one does find greater peace of mind and heart.

For those who are in this process, there is also the question of, the need for, the alleviation of suffering. When people are sick, they turn to the monastery, and the monastery responds with, for example, liturgical services, healing services. Each day we do a healing service. In these services, the whole community directs its energy to helping people in need. This helps not only those in need but helps the community grow in its compassion and loving kindness. We also perform priestly bedside services, counsel the family, particularly when death is imminent. We give support to people who are housebound or handicapped. We sometimes provide legal aid and financial support, housecleaning and baby-sitting, transportation and shopping. These activities are the ten thousand hands of great compassion, alleviating human suffering.

Then there is the transformation of suffering. At the deep level of our spiritual life, we dedicate ourselves to transforming our suffering for the compassionate healing of the world.

There are ways in which, in the very midst of our suffering and troubles, we can administer compassionate healing to others. This transforms our suffering into a skillful means of caring for others, and when we do this, we can find peace in our own suffering condition. In this regard, we have the following *koan*:

> The great Master Dogen, who is the founder of our Soto Zen lineage, was ill. A monk said to him, "Master, you are not feeling well. Is there anyone who doesn't get sick?"
>
> Dogen replied, "Yes, there is."
>
> The monk responded, "Does the person who doesn't get sick take care of you?"
>
> Dogen said, "I have the opportunity to take care of that person."
>
> The monk asked, "What happens when you take care of that person?"
>
> Dogen answered, "At that time I am unable to see my sickness."

# CHAPTER TWO

# His Holiness Tenzin Gyatso the Fourteenth Dalai Lama

## THE TRANSFORMATION OF SUFFERING

**His Holiness the Dalai Lama**
Regarding the transformation of suffering, our Buddhist texts on logic explain that every single phenomenon has countless aspects. So, much depends on the angle from which you view something. For example, when you encounter suffering, if you dwell only on its painful aspects, it is intolerable. But if you forget that aspect, you may be able to see it from another angle. The Buddhist point of view is that by enduring suffering, you can

purify your past negative actions and generate the determination to achieve liberation.

Therefore, it is not true to say that suffering remains the same from any angle. The nature of suffering changes, depending on your mental attitude and the way you look at it. If you are able to transform adverse situations into factors of the spiritual path, hindrances will become favorable conditions for spiritual practice. Through accustoming your mind to such a practice, you will meet with success and nothing will hinder your spiritual progress. It is said that being able to transmute adverse situations in this way is a sign that you are really undergoing spiritual training.

Taking adverse situations onto the path can be done in various ways. In good times or bad times, whether we are rich or poor, happy or unhappy, whether we are staying in our own or a foreign country, in a village, a city, a monastery, or an isolated place, whoever is accompanying us, whatever kinds of suffering we encounter, we can reflect that there are many other sentient beings encountering similar sufferings. And we can go on to think: "May the suffering I am undergoing serve to counter the sufferings experienced by other sentient beings. May they be parted from suffering."

The primary aim of the meditational practice of taking on others' sufferings is to eliminate our self-centered attitude. If you apply it with dedication, you will find it effective. The practice of taking on the suffering of others is one of the most forceful techniques for controlling self-centeredness.

To motivate ourselves, we can think about the plight of suffering beings on the one hand and the benefits of compassion on the other. Like us, other beings are under the influence of disturbing emotions, such as ignorance, desire, animosity, and jealousy. Consequently, they cannot enjoy the happiness they wish for but constantly suffer varieties of pain.

Compassion, on the other hand, is crucial to our survival as human beings wherever we live. We human beings are social animals. We need companions to survive. If we develop concern for other people's welfare, share other people's suffering, and help them, ultimately we will benefit. If we think only of ourselves and forget about others, ultimately we will lose. The more we care for the happiness of others, the greater our own sense of well-being becomes. Cultivating a close, warm-hearted feeling for others automatically puts the mind at ease. This helps remove whatever fears or insecurities we may have and gives us the strength to cope with any obstacles we may encounter. It is the ultimate source of success in life.

### Venerable Thubten Chodron

What His Holiness the Dalai Lama is suggesting relates to a practice in Tibetan Buddhism called taking and giving. It is where we imagine taking on the suffering of others and using it to destroy the cause of our own suffering, which is our own self-grasping ignorance and our own self-centeredness. Then we imagine transforming and giving away our body, our possessions, and our positive potential to all sentient beings, which brings them happiness. We meditate in this way to overcome our own obstacles that prevent us from being of benefit to others when the situation arises in which we can be of benefit to others.

### Geshe Lhundub Sopa

The practice of taking and giving is one of His Holiness the Dalai Lama's favorites. Shantideva, the great Buddhist saint and teacher, says that all the violence and suffering we cause to ourselves and others comes from the mind. They arise due to the fact that we put ourselves first. We cherish ourselves first, and then we may love our parents and children and many kinds of things, but always with ourselves in mind. This kind of egoism comes from the mind and when lived out dominates the world around us, causing suffering for everyone. The devil in egoism is our insecurity, our sense of worthlessness, our pride, our fears—all these afflictive emotions. So, the most important practice in any religion is the one that makes us less self-centered and more cherishing of others. This is why His Holiness the Dalai Lama prefers the practice of taking and giving.

### Geshe Lobsang Tenzin

The practice of taking and giving is done as a way to reinforce one's compassion and love for others. It helps us become like a mother who very much cares for her child. If a mother's child is inflicted with a certain pain or suffering, she would want to take that suffering upon herself. So in that sense, the practice of taking and giving is transformative. It transforms our own self-centeredness, our selfishness, that prevents us from seeking the happiness of others and sharing our happiness with others. This kind of compassion is certainly a powerful antidote to the troubled world we live in today.

Someone may ask, "But can you really take away the suffering of others? Can you erase their negative karma?" Of course, there may be various interpretations. In Tibetan Buddhism, we often reply by citing a verse that says:

> *The Buddhas cannot wash away sins or negative karma of others as if washing dirt with water.*
> *They cannot remove the suffering of others as if simply sweeping away the dust from the floor.*
> *They cannot transfer their realizations directly into other people's minds, other beings' lives.*
> *They lead the beings to liberation by showing them reality.*

Nobody can really erase the suffering or karma of others. But by living compassionately with others, we can lead others to a path by which they can transform their own negative karma and thereby overcome suffering and attain peace and happiness.

## Reverend Heng Sure

His Holiness the Dalai Lama is speaking from the point of view of the bodhisattva, the bodhisattva's path. A bodhisattva is a person who seeks awakening in order to better care for others. In the *Flower Ornament Sutra,* it says that taking on the suffering of others is the highest form of offering. Now, it is also true that each person's karma is his or hers to pay back, good and bad. However, we vow to save all living beings, no matter how numberless. Because there is personal karma and collective karma, we are all participating in both of those, right this minute. So, someone who makes a resolve to end suffering on behalf of others is at the same time creating his or her own personal karma but also working on the level of collective karma. At this collective level, we can greatly benefit others by our good deeds.

※

## Abbot John Daido Loori

In our Zen lineage we understand atonement as at-one-ment, nonduality. So to atone, for example, for our evil karma, we become intimate with it; that is, we take responsibility for that karma. And in so doing, we are able to transform it.

I feel that His Holiness the Dalai Lama is saying that the same process is taking place in terms of being intimate with the suffering of others. By being intimate with others' suffering, we can take the responsibility to help to transform them.

We chant, "Sentient beings are numberless. I vow to save them." Well, the way you save sentient beings is to recognize that self and other are one reality. And when you do that, there is no longer the duality that creates the self as separate from others. So the self disappears in a sense and merges with the ten thousand things, with the whole phenomenal universe.

The *Prajnaparamita Sutras* speak of the relative, the absolute, and the merging of those realities. In terms of the relative reality, you and I are different. The absolute reality is the non-dual basis in which you and I are the same. Finally, we are the same thing, but I'm not you and you are not me. And both of those facts exist simultaneously, at least from the Mahayana perspective. Let me clarify this.

Master Dogen teaches that all things are Buddha-nature. When we return to our True Self, our Buddha-nature, we understand that when any being suffers, we suffer. Their suffering is my suffering because ultimately there is no distinction between me and them. It is with this enlightened insight that we can share the suffering of others and truly work to bring peace and happiness to all living beings.

*Ajahn Amaro*
One of the very common practices in the Buddhist tradition is something known as sharing of blessings or sharing of merit. It is not exactly atoning for another person's wrongdoings, but

it's a way of consciously sending forth your good intentions and benevolent wishes; if you like, sharing the good karma of your own life to benefit others.

This is a major part of Buddhist practice in all Buddhist countries. So when a wholesome act is done, and when there is a conscious committal of that act and its effects for the benefit of an individual or group of individuals, it is not seen as wiping out another person's negative karma. But it is seen as an amelioration of the painful effects that they are experiencing or of a difficult situation that they are in. This kind of caring for others is certainly at the heart of our practice. His Holiness is bringing that to our attention because its emphasis is so needed today.

*Venerable Henepola Gunaratana*
Whether we follow the Theravada or the Mahayana Buddhist traditions, we all practice what are called the Four Sublime States of Mind: loving friendliness, compassion, appreciative joy, and equanimity. This is not a personal selfish practice. When we practice loving friendliness, we practice loving friendliness for all living beings, humans as well as nonhumans. Similarly with compassion, appreciative joy, and equanimity, we practice in order to liberate all living beings from suffering. Therefore, in this sense we commit our wholesome individual

and collective karma for all beings. So, I think in this light that what His Holiness the Dalai Lama has mentioned is a very wonderful and effective statement.

### Samu Sunim

I think His Holiness the Dalai Lama is trying to point out the need for balance, striking a balance between reconciliation with the past on one hand and creating a new hope or a new future on the other.

He uses the word "endurance." In Buddhism, endurance is involved in both purification and prevention. Buddhists use the term "endurance" to describe something that is essential to purification. Given that we have done unwholesome things in the past, we must endure the consequences. We have to be accountable and responsible. So, we have to endure purification in reconciling with the past.

At the same time, we have to make sure that unwholesome actions do not happen again in different forms. To do this we have to endure the difficulties of building a more hopeful environment. For example, today we are concerned about terrorism, and rightly so, but we need to distinguish between retaliatory and preventive actions. Retaliation would perpetuate unwholesome actions, just in different forms. The scenario would go on and on. Preventive action protects and at the same time creates a new peaceful and prosperous environment for everyone, creating new hope for the future. This kind of prevention is more difficult and needs our endurance.

As we endure suffering, we need to realize, with wisdom and compassion for ourselves and others, that purification is taking place. We also need to use wisdom and compassion to actively build a new and hopeful future for ourselves and for others. These two need to be in balance in the transformation of suffering. I see a call for that balance in the words of His Holiness the Dalai Lama.

### Zenkei Blanche Hartman

I believe that His Holiness the Dalai Lama is offering this teaching to us because it is exactly a practice that anyone can do anywhere, anytime: taking on the suffering of others and giving out well-being and happiness.

I'd like to tell you about a student of mine, who suffers from anger. She generally goes around in a resentful kind of mind-set. She has just been learning the practice of taking and giving. One day, as she saw a woman struggling to cross the street ahead of her because of some deformity, she began to practice taking and giving with this woman.

Now, what effect it had on the woman's suffering after being helped across the street, I have no idea. But the effect that it had on my student's suffering was dramatic. By the time she got across the street and got in her car, she experienced a flood of gratitude for her life, which she had never expressed to me before. When we choose to love others, the love transforms our lives. It brings us the peace for which we are looking. So this is why, I think, His Holiness is asking us to consider this practice, and to offer it to others.

# CHAPTER THREE

# His Holiness
# Pope John Paul II

## THE MEANING OF SUFFERING

*His Holiness Pope John Paul II*
Even though personal suffering seems almost inexpressible and not transferable, perhaps at the same time nothing else requires as much to be dealt with, meditated upon, and conceived as an explicit problem. Human suffering is multidimensional. People suffer in different ways that are wider than sickness and more deeply rooted in humanity itself. We can see this in the distinction between physical and moral suffering.

In the Hebrew Scripture, a few examples of situations that bear the signs of suffering are: the danger of death, the death of one's own children, the lack of offspring, nostalgia for one's homeland, persecution and hostility, mockery and scorn, loneliness and abandonment, the remorse of conscience, the unfaithfulness and ingratitude of friends and neighbors, and the misfortunes of one's own nation. While suffering has a subjective and a passive character, in the psychological sense it is also marked by the activity of generating such feelings as sadness, disappointment, discouragement, or even despair.

It can be said that these experiences of suffering are connected to a kind of evil. Evil is a certain lack, limitation, or distortion of good. We could say that people suffer because of a good in which they do not share, from which in a certain sense they are cut off or of which they have deprived themselves. People particularly suffer when they "ought" to have a share in a good and do not have it.

Within each form of suffering endured by people, there inevitably arises the question: Why? In brief, it is a question about the meaning of suffering. A person who asks this question suffers in a humanly speaking still deeper way if he or she does not find a satisfactory answer to this question. Yet as with Job, innocent suffering must be accepted as a mystery, which the individual is unable to penetrate completely by his or her own intelligence.

Love is also the richest source of the meaning of suffering, which always remains a mystery. In the New Testament, Christ causes us to enter into the mystery and to discover the "why" of suffering, as far as we are capable of grasping the sublimity of divine love. Love is also the fullest source of the answer to the question of the meaning of suffering. This answer has been given by God to humankind in the cross of Jesus Christ.

Jesus says to Nicodemus that God "so loved the world" that he gives his only begotten Son so that humankind "should not perish." The meaning of these words is precisely specified by the words that follow, "but have eternal life" (John 3:16). Jesus is given to humanity primarily to protect people against this definitive evil and against definitive suffering. He conquers sin by his obedience unto death, and he overcomes death by his resurrection. Death constitutes, as it were, a definitive summing up of the destructive work both in the bodily organism and in the psyche. Death primarily involves the dissolution of the entire psychophysical personality of the human person. Jesus blots out from human history the dominion of sin and, by his resurrection, begins the process of the future resurrection of the body. Both are essential conditions of "eternal life," that is, of humanity's definitive happiness in union with God. Even though the victory over sin and death achieved by Christ in his cross and resurrection does not abolish temporal suffering from human life, it nevertheless throws a new light upon every suffering: the light of salvation.

Jesus Christ entered the world of human suffering. In his public activity, he experienced fatigue, homelessness, misunderstanding, and became progressively more and more isolated and encircled by hostility. In his passion, he experienced: arrest, humiliation, blows and spitting, contempt for the prisoner, an unjust sentence, scourging, crowning with thorns, mocking, carrying the cross, crucifixion, and agony. Even more, he, though innocent, took upon himself the sufferings of all people, because he took upon himself the sins of all: "For our sake he made him to be sin who knew no sin" (2 Corinthians 5:21). The man of sorrows is truly the "Lamb of God who takes away the sin of the world" (John 1:29).

Christ gives the answer to the question about suffering and the meaning of suffering not only by his teachings but most of all by his own suffering. When Christ says, "My God, my God, why have you abandoned me?" his words express the suffering that is the estrangement from God. But precisely through this suffering he accomplishes the redemption. Human suffering has reached its culmination in the passion of Christ. At the same time, it has entered into a completely new dimension and a new order: It has been linked to love. In the cross of Christ, we must also pose anew the question about the meaning of suffering and read in the cross, to its very depths, the answer to this question.

In the cross of Christ, not only is the redemption accomplished through suffering but also human suffering itself has been redeemed. In bringing about the redemption through suffering, Christ has raised human suffering to the level of the redemption. Thus each person in his or her suffering can become a sharer in the redemptive suffering of Christ. Paul speaks about "sharing abundantly in the sufferings of Christ" (2 Corinthians 1:5). If one becomes a sharer in the sufferings of Christ, this happens because Christ has opened his suffering to humankind, because he himself in his redemptive suffering has become in a certain sense a sharer in all human suffering.

So, people can rediscover Christ's sufferings in their own

sufferings, giving them new meaning. Suffering, in fact, is always a trial—at times a very hard one—to which humanity is subjected. But those who share in Christ's sufferings have before their eyes the paschal mystery of the cross and resurrection. We see this in Paul's words, "We are . . . fellow heirs with Christ, provided we suffer with him in order that we may also be glorified with him" (Romans 8:17). Or, "Now I rejoice in my sufferings for your sake, and in my flesh I complete what is lacking in Christ's afflictions for the sake of his body, that is, the church" (Colossians 1:24).

The sufferings of Christ created the good of the world's redemption. No person can add anything to it. But at the same time, Christ has in a sense opened his own redemptive suffering to all human suffering. Insofar as a person becomes a sharer in Christ's sufferings, to that extent he or she completes the suffering through which Christ accomplished the redemption of the world. This does not mean that the redemption achieved by Christ is not complete. It only means that the redemption remains always open to all love expressed in human suffering. In Christ's redemptive suffering, he opened himself to every human suffering and constantly does so. This redemption lives on and in its own special way develops in the history of humankind. In this dimension, every human suffering, by reason of the loving union with Christ, completes the suffering of Christ, just as the church completes the redemptive work of Christ.

The interior process in which a person discovers the meaning of suffering often begins and is set in motion with great difficulty. Nevertheless, it takes time, even a long time, for the answer to begin to be interiorly perceived. People hear Christ's saving answer as they gradually become sharers in the sufferings of Christ. The answer that comes in this way is something more than the mere abstract answer to the question of the meaning of suffering. For it is above all a call: "Follow me!" Come! Take part through your suffering in this work of saving the world, a salvation achieved through my suffering! Through my cross. Gradually, as the individual takes up his or her cross, spiritually uniting himself or herself to the cross of Christ, the salvific meaning of suffering is revealed. It is then that a person finds in his or her suffering interior peace and even spiritual joy. Paul speaks of such joy: "I rejoice in my sufferings for your sake" (Colossians 1:24).

The parable of the Good Samaritan belongs to the gospel of suffering. For it indicates what the relationship of each of us must be toward our suffering neighbor. Therefore, one must cultivate a sensitivity of heart, which bears witness to compassion toward a suffering person. Nevertheless, the Good Samaritan of Christ's parable does not stop at sympathy and compassion alone. They become for him an incentive to actions aimed at bringing help to the injured person. Unselfish love stirs the heart and actions. The value of Christian love of neighbor forms a framework to combat various forms of hatred, violence, cruelty, or insensitivity toward one's neighbor and his or her suffering.

Christ's revelation of the salvific meaning of suffering is in no way identified with an attitude of passivity. Completely the reverse is true. We remember those disturbing words of the Final Judgment:

*Come, O blessed of my Father, inherit the kingdom prepared for you from the foundation of the world: for I was hungry and you gave me food, I was thirsty and you gave me drink, I was a stranger and you welcomed me, I was in prison and you came to me. . . . Truly, I say to you, as you did it to one of the least of these my brethren, you did it to me* (Matthew 25:34–36, 40).

Christ himself is present in every suffering person without exception, since his salvific suffering has been opened once and for all to every human suffering. Suffering in the world is the opportunity to release love, to give birth to works of love toward neighbor, in order to transform the whole human civilization into a "civilization of love." In this love the salvific meaning of suffering is completely accomplished and reaches its definitive dimension. At one and the same time, Christ has taught us to do good by our suffering and to do good to those who suffer. In this double aspect he has completely revealed the meaning of suffering.

# CHAPTER FOUR

# The Wisdom
# of the Cross

*Father Donald Grabner*
The passover of Christ himself as he passed
through his passion, suffering, and death to
the resurrection is seen as the prototype and
the cause of all other passovers. This passover
of Christ points to, and is a pledge of, what
every Christian looks to in his or her own life.
While we understand Christ's suffering to be
vicarious, in that he takes our sins upon himself and sacrifices himself as the paschal lamb
who redemptively dies for us, nevertheless it's
also an example that we are to follow. In other
words, we are to imitate Christ himself in the
sense that we see our whole life as this same

kind of a passing over from death to life, with all that this implies.

In our Christian monastic tradition, we are offered many ways by which we are to incarnate the paschal mystery in our own lives. To use a common Buddhist term, one could call these ways "skillful means." In my own monastic life, the most useful aid that I have found for this has been the liturgy of the paschal mystery that we celebrate in a special way annually during the three days of Good Friday, Holy Saturday, and Easter Sunday and that is also celebrated in each and every Eucharist. It's this passover mystery that the liturgy attempts to embed in our daily existence. It's mysterious because there is something about it that simply cannot be expressed in words. There comes a certain point in which we have an experience that is ineffable, because somehow it's God at work rather than some finite element about which we could really talk.

This liturgical skillful means is accompanied by many others. One of the most important is the practice of *lectio divina,* that is, our contemplative reading of the Scriptures and commentaries on the Scriptures. There is also the example that the monks give to one another through their own ways of approaching suffering and death. In our life in community, where we have the young and the old living together, the old are able to offer what our abbot sometimes calls the "apostolate of suffering," by which they witness the positive aspects of suffering to other members of the community as well as to persons who come to see us.

This can be a hard lesson, for many of the sick and the elderly can be demanding and impatient. These are the ones who, as St. Benedict says in his *Rule,* really require from the community patience and tolerance, because they are the ones who are most in need. Happily, there will always be those among the elders—and I hope eventually to be one of this kind myself—who are preeminent models of patience. Their ability to let go is an inspiration to the entire community. Let me mention two examples of what I mean.

First, there was the striking example of our Brother Julius, an uneducated man whose work for the monastery had been primarily that of manual labor on the farm and in the kitchen. Suddenly incapacitated by emphysema and forced to take up permanent residence in the infirmary, he not only remained relentlessly cheerful but also, in his own inarticulate manner, fashioned for us a living apostolate of suffering. His simple piety was built on the conviction that his suffering was redemptive not only for himself but also for others because he was able to join it to the suffering of Christ.

Likewise, our Father Luke in his later years contracted a serious illness followed by an extremely painful form of facial neuralgia. Although in his early life he had certain ways of doing things that some of his confreres found hard to tolerate, when he moved to the infirmary and was almost totally dependent on the care of his brother monks, he became an outstanding model of patience and acceptance. These outstanding examples of patiently enduring illness and old age lead us, of course, to reflect on our own advancing years and help us face head-on the realities that lie ahead for us.

### Father Daniel Ward

When I was a young priest-monk, a monk who was older than I was in age but younger in the religious vocation once came to speak with me. He told me that he wanted to talk with me because he had seen how at various times I had been crushed in community but was still there. He himself was then being crushed both by the abbot, who did not like him, and the university institution, which did not want him. He was really on the cross.

My response at the time was that I accepted everything that goes with the monastic life, including suffering, because all I wanted to be was a monk. At that time, I had little understanding beyond the status of a monk and the optimism of youth. I could suffer personally because I wanted to be a monk. But the more I grew as a monk, the more I understood that having the status of a monk and being young would not sustain me in dealing with troubling situations—nor was it the monastic way. Most of all, I realized that I continued to hold deep within me the pain, hurts, and insecurities of my life. More than anyone or anything, I was violent toward myself and was suffering for it.

The answer to transforming my personal suffering—the suffering harbored for years within me as well as the suffering caused by other persons and institutions—was not found in what the monastery itself did to alleviate my suffering but in what the monastic way taught to be the journey of the monk and the tools that it offered to walk that journey. Perhaps the enlightenment came to me while I was administrator of an abbey. Because of both inner and outer baggage that need not be related here, I was filled with pain. I had inwardly collapsed. But I continued to engage in monastic practices, especially silence and *lectio divina,* the sacred reading of Scripture. What I discovered in Scripture was the phrase "patient endurance." This became my mantra and my understanding of the way of the cross.

In our spirituality, patient endurance is not passive but active. It takes hold of my suffering so that it does not destroy me. Patient endurance is quietly and patiently devictimizing myself and refusing to be part of the cycle of victimization. Patient endurance means not to accept being a victim. Rather, it is about overcoming the suffering, the victimization, by not joining with it, continuing it, or inflicting it on myself or others.

The monastic way of the cross, then, teaches that it is not the cloister or the routine that heals the inner pain but rather the inner journey that a person embarks on through prayer, silence, and reading. This journey helps one harmonize God, creation, and self. This journey leads through suffering into this harmony. I have found this to be true as I am sustained by the quiet inner way of my journey, the way I come to connect with creation, God, and myself.

### Father William Skudlarek

At Mass one day, the monk who was the main celebrant recalled that on that date fifteen years before we had celebrated Good Friday, the day when Christians commemorate the death of Christ. He also said that that was the very day on which Abbot James Fox died and that Abbot Fox's motto was *Deus crucifixus,* God crucified. He further recalled that forty years ago, when he made his first vows as a Trappist monk, it was Dom James who preached in his homily, "No one is saved except through suffering." He actually repeated it five times in that homily: "No one is saved except through suffering."

As I heard these remarks at Mass that morning, I kept thinking, "But we want to be saved *from* suffering, don't we?" The paradoxical truth is that we are saved from suffering through suffering. In the patient acceptance of suffering, we find the key to the transformation of suffering into the deeper life we are seeking.

### Father Kevin Hunt

When I had recently entered the monastery and was learning to be a monk, I was sent down to the garden with other young monks. Our job that day was to plant rhubarb. The monk in charge of the garden told me to dig a line of holes a foot and a half deep and about a foot wide. Somebody else drove a tractor with a wagon attached along the line of holes. In the wagon was a pile of fresh manure. One of the other brothers placed a large shovelful of manure into the holes.

There I was, a young man just out of New York City, who considered himself to be rather sophisticated. I looked into the hole with its mess of manure and got kind of sick to my stomach. The brother in charge of the work passed by and said, "Well, get to it." I asked, "What should I do?" He replied, "Just throw some dirt on the manure and mix it up with your hands. When you put the root into the hole and fill it in, the manure is going to fertilize and compost it."

Most of us who engage in religious practice tend to be very idealistic. We just do not want things to be messy. The truth is that in this life, the messiness is always with us. We are never going to get rid of it. And it's the willingness to have this messiness in our lives that is going to carry us to where our seeds can really grow.

### Reverend Heng Sure

From a Buddhist point of view, suffering can be seen as the compost of discarded wrong thoughts, feelings, and actions that produces the seed of awakening. Out of the discarded leaves and stalks and thorns comes that seed of true fruit. As I first came around the corner in the road and saw Gethsemani Abbey, just so dramatic, popping up there and striking the eye, I thought, "What a great compost heap that is!" Let me explain.

Monastics are drawn in the Buddhist case to the *Vinaya* (monastic precepts) and in the Benedictine case to the *Rule* of St. Benedict. There is compassion in these moral guides, which comes from wisdom. Those guides in the *Rule* and the *Vinaya* present compassionate ways to compost all of the stuff that arises from our humanity—the greed, hatred, stupidity, pride, and doubt—putting them on the compost heap so that through the monastic forms of compassion and wisdom, something new can be born.

### Geshe Lobsang Tenzin

In the Buddhist tradition of spiritual development, it's not that suffering itself is embraced for the sake of suffering. Just embracing it is not completing the journey. But embracing suffering, or understanding suffering, provides a way to discover where the suffering originates. It is also through embracing our sufferings that we understand other people's feelings.

Shantideva has a way of saying that without suffering, there is no will to freedom. The Buddhist would look, in this regard, at the very life of Buddha. It was at the point where he was able to see the suffering of aging, sickness, and death that he would face and others were facing that he discovered that he was very much connected with others. And this led him to want to find where this shared suffering originates.

What the Buddha realized at the end of his search for the

origin of suffering is that suffering, or unhappiness, is simply the product of our misconceptions, not knowing our true reality. Now, in this regard, it may seem paradoxical to talk about our true reality on one hand and having no self on the other. But it is not so paradoxical if we remember that in Buddhist Madhyamika philosophy, you find two levels of reality: the conventional reality and the ultimate reality of oneself, and of every phenomenon for that matter.

Emptiness is the ultimate reality of every phenomenon. That is to say, each individual has no core self that separates him or her from the rest of the universe. It is the clinging to a notion that one is an independent individual that leads one to make oneself the center of one's universe. Clinging to that misconception of oneself is where the basic duality, the "concrete me versus the concrete others" comes from. And from this come the forms of suffering and unhappiness we experience in our daily lives. But dissolving that sense of independent selfhood is not about dissolving the self altogether. It simply means understanding ourselves in a different way, in a relational sense or in a dependent manner.

The Buddhist's way to freedom begins with embracing our suffering existence, our unhappiness, not running away from it into different diversions. Embracing suffering opens our eyes to our common humanity and moves us to discover where our shared suffering comes from. The gradual deepening of our understanding of our true nature, and how we have created our independent self-identity and are clinging to it, connects us to the world in a way that brings true happiness.

But we need to realize this truth about ourselves at an experimental level, not just at a conceptual level. It is at this deeper level of direct experience that we find a connection with everyone and everything. There, the Buddhist would say, we find enlightenment, freedom from grasping the self, and, ultimately, an infinite love and compassion for all in the deepest sense of connectedness with all.

### Father Kevin Hunt

I remember an incident when I was with a group of monastics that had gone over to India to visit different Tibetan monasteries. We were up in Dharamsala and there met a monk who had come out from Tibet a couple of weeks or months before. He had spent, if I remember correctly, well over twenty years in a Chinese prison in Lhasa.

As we were talking, he began to cry because I had asked him, "What was the greatest suffering that you had?" And he said, "There I was with other monks, and we were all very well educated." They were all *geshes,* highly learned monks, and he said, "The thing that terrorized me the most was to see the number who had given up in despair." He said it was not uncommon for people to be driven to the end of their rope and to take a way out in some form of suicide. And he said, "That really shook me because traditionally we had all the answers. We had gone through all of the mental exercises. We had attained deep insights. But when it came down to it, the suffering was beyond the capacity of the insights to give a solution."

So I finally asked him, "Well, what was it that finally enabled you to survive?" And he replied, "I just gave myself to the suffering, with no thought, just gave myself to the suffering." I immediately thought, "Jesus Christ."

### Father Thomas Keating

I appreciate the many insights that come on the spiritual journey, whether in Buddhism or Christianity. But these insights are not the goal of the journey. I have been wondering whether in the Buddhist tradition there is something that corresponds to what in the Christian contemplative heritage is called the dark night. This is a passive purification by which, without effort of our own except to quiet the mind or shut off the interior dialogue, we become vulnerable to the contents of the unconscious. Then the repressed material that is talked about in depth psychology begins to emerge in the form of painful or primitive emotions that bombard our consciousness. This kind of purification is much more important than religious experiences, for the goal of this purification is a permanent state of freedom from the false self.

I once was conferring with Trungpa Rinpoche, and I raised the following question with him: "In the Christian scheme of

things, we believe that there is a normally intense spiritual suffering that one needs to pass through to reach union, and especially unity with God. Is there something similar in your
tradition?" And he said, "Oh yes, we have a word for that. We
call it *old-dog spirituality.*"

I was fascinated by this term. What I understood by the image of an old dog is one that has been reduced to a state of ut-
ter powerlessness. All it can do is lie around most of the day,
get up maybe once or twice, wag its tail, have a sip of water or
eat something, and lie down again. It's the radical experience
of powerlessness or, if you prefer, nothingness, in the process
of spiritual purification. This is the level, it seems to me, to
which our practice should bring us. And it is only a great love
of the spiritual journey and of the Ultimate Reality that can
lead one to put up with this kind of suffering through which
one must pass to reach the true goal of the spiritual life.

### Father Columba Stewart

While it is true that much of our suffering is caused by ourselves, many of us also find ourselves caught up in war, or personal devastation, or sexual abuse, or you name it. That's not
suffering that I am creating for myself. It's coming at me from
somewhere else. But whether suffering comes from within or
without, it is not easily understood.

Evagrius, a fourth-century monk to whom I often turn as a

teacher, once said, "When we pray, we have to make our stand on our own desolation." When our heart takes our suffering into itself and makes it prayer, it is transformed and contributes to growth in the spiritual life. One of St. Benedict's steps of humility is "The heart quietly embraces suffering." When our heart gently wraps itself around our suffering condition, the problem may not be resolved, but it becomes a part of our spiritual path that requires us to go ahead and not dwell on the suffering itself.

In Iris Murdoch's lovely novel *The Bell,* there is a wise abbess who gives counsel to a man who is troubled by what is today the quite apropos and relevant issue of sexual attraction to a minor. And the abbess's advice to this man is this: "The way is always forward. Never back." This sounds like a classic saying from any one of our traditions, and it's one that we need to hold on to.

Finally, in regard to this journey and the suffering it entails, it is important to remember that in the accounts of Jesus' great passion on the way to the resurrection, there is a time between when they put him in the freshly made tomb and when the tomb is found to be empty. Many of us can at times find ourselves in that period of hiatus between the cross and any clear evidence of resurrection. This is a time when we don't have a lot of explicit clues as to what is happening in the inner workings of our own transformation. But the key point is that it does happen. Benedict allows for experiences of transformation in this life, but he is cautious about confusing what happens here with eternal life that we experience in heaven.

### Sister Kathy Lyzotte

On the question of where God is in all the suffering of the world, this past Lent for noon reading in our monastery, we had the book by Sheila Cassidy entitled *Good Friday People*. In that book, Cassidy quotes Elie Wiesel, who had been in a concentration camp during World War II and had seen a young child on a gallows struggling and dying. Somebody in the crowd said, "Where is God now?" Wiesel heard a voice within answering, "God is here, hanging here on this gallows," in this child who is dying. God is revealed, becomes manifest as the Suffering Servant in the midst of suffering, in the very person who is suffering.

It is also my belief, our Christian belief, that God is present as the suffering Christ in each one of us who suffers. We can find God in the suffering. That discovery gives us great consolation and opens us to the sacred in our darkness and pain.

### Father Joseph Wong

Concerning finding God amid all the suffering and conflicts in the world, perhaps we Christians would not tend to say in the abstract that God is present but would rather say that Jesus Christ is present, the suffering Christ. There is an interesting episode in the Catholic devotion known as the Way of the Cross. According to tradition, a pious woman named Veronica, seeing Jesus carrying the cross with so much suffering, had the courage to approach him. With her veil she wiped the face of Jesus, and his suffering image remained on the veil, the famous veil of Veronica.

Caryll Houselander, a spiritual writer, has a beautiful reflection about this veil in her book *The Comforting of Christ*. She wrote: "The veil of Veronica, which bears the suffering image of Christ, is not only kept in the museum, but is now found in the entire world." Suffering humanity has become that veil of Veronica, bearing the suffering image of Christ whenever there is human suffering: children being abused, people suffering from AIDS or cancer or other illness, violence, war, and so on. The whole world, wherever there is suffering, reflects the image of Christ left on the veil of Veronica. It's truly Jesus Christ present in those who suffer, Jesus continuing to suffer in solidarity with suffering humanity.

Recall that when Saul, who later became Paul, was on the way to Damascus and Jesus appeared to him, he asked, "Saul, Saul, why are you persecuting me?" Saul was persecuting the Christians, but the question was "Why are you persecuting *me*?" So, too, we believe that Christ even today is present in the suffering people and continues to suffer in solidarity with them.

# CHAPTER FIVE

# Abandonment and

# Love

*Ewert H. Cousins*
My conviction is that the greatest image of suffering and alienation in Christianity occurs just before the death of Christ on the cross, when he cries out, "My God, my God, why have you forsaken me?" This is a tremendous statement of emptiness. It is incredible! Eventually he dies on the cross. But the drama does not end there. On the third day, he rises from the dead. I think that these two dynamics—absolute alienation followed by absolute transformation—are the energies that have supported Christians through the centuries.

### Father Leo Lefebure

There are different ways of reading "My God, my God, why have you forsaken me?" One way is that it is literally a cry of despair. On that model for Christians, Jesus as God himself is entering into the worst depth of human suffering. This means that God knows what it's like to feel abandoned by God. This also means a divine identification with all the victims of suffering throughout history, with all those who have in their suffering felt a sense of God-forsakenness, of feeling that God is not there.

But we should also remember that this cry of Jesus quotes Psalm 22. It was a custom in Judaism at the time that if one person said the first line of a psalm, the rest of the people would conclude it. This is like when a Catholic says, "Our Father," and everybody else joins in. So, given that the Twenty-second Psalm begins with this cry of despair but moves through it and concludes with a sense of God's deliverance, there is a message of suffering and transformation that we all are invited to repeat following the model of Jesus.

### Zoketsu Norman Fischer

I've been spending time with the psalms. And from my reading of Psalm 22, what I get out of these words of abandonment is that they express a profound and total acceptance of suffering. He is taking responsibility for his suffering, becoming it with his whole body and mind. In the crying out, there is a sense of being heard. The feeling of being heard effects the transformation. The sense of being heard and held in the deepest of all possible human suffering effects the liberation. The path of the cross here is to completely give up any resistance whatsoever to the suffering and to be met in that acceptance.

Having said that, here is my own version of Psalm 22:

*My God, my God, why have you forsaken me?*
*Why so far from my delivery*
*So empty in the anguish of my words?*
*I call to you in the daytime but you don't answer*
*And all night long I plead restlessly, uselessly*

*I know your holiness, find it in the memorized praises*
*Uttered by those who've struggled with you*
*Through all the generations*
*These, my forebears, trusted you*
*And through their trusting you touched them*
*Held and delivered them*
*They cried out to you and you met them face to face*
*Their confidence was strong and they were not confounded*

*But I am not as they*
*Utterly alone, I am cast out of the circle*
*A worm, a living reproach, scorned and despised, even less*
  *than despised*
*Unheard, unseen, unacknowledged, denied*
*And all who encounter me revile me with cynic Laughter*

*Shaking their heads, parting their nattering lips, Mocking*
*"Let him throw himself at God for his deliverance," they say*
*"Since that is who he trusts let the Lord save him."*

*And they are right:*
*How not trust you, and what else to trust?*

*You I entered on leaving the womb*
*You I drank at my mother's breast*
*I was cast upon you at birth*
*And even before birth I swam in you, my heart's darkness*

*Be not far from me now*
*When suffering is very near*
*And there is no help*
*And I am beset all round by threatening powers*
*The bulls of Bashan gaping their dismal braying mouths*
*Their ravenous roaring lion mouths*

*I am poured out like water*
*My bones' joints are snapped like twigs*
*My heart melts like wax*
*Flooding my bowels with searing viscid emotion*
*My strength is dried up like a potsherd*
*My tongue cleaves woolly to the roof of my mouth*
*And I feel my body dissolving into death's dusts*

*For I am hounded by my isolation*
*Am cast off and encircled by the assembly of the violent*

*Who like vicious dogs snap at my hands and feet*
*I count the bones of my naked body*
*As the mongrels shift and stare and circle*
*They divide my clothes among themselves, casting lots for them*

*So now in this very place I call on you*
*There is no one left*

*Do not be far from me*
*Be the center*
*Of the center*
*Of the circle*
*Be the strength of that center*
*The power of the absence that is the center*
*Deliver my life from the killing sharpnesses*
*Deliver my soul from the feverish dogs*
*Save me from the lion mouths*
*Answer me with the voice of the ram's horn*
*And I will seek and form and repeat your name among my*
*    kinsmen*
*In the midst of everyone I will compose praises with my lips*
*And those who enter your awesomeness through my words will*
*    also praise*
*All the seed of Jacob will glorify you*
*And live in awe of you*
*All those who question and struggle*
*Will dawn with your light*
*For they will know*
*You have not scorned the poor and despised*

*Nor recoiled disgusted from their faces*
*From them your spark has never been hidden*
*And when they cried out in their misery*
*You heard and answered and ennobled them*
*And it is the astonishment of this that I will praise in the*
*    Great Assembly*
*Making deep vows in the presence of those who know your*
*    heart*
*Know that in you the meek eat and are satisfied*
*And all who seek and struggle find the tongue to praise*
*Saying to you:*

*May your heart live forever*
*May all the ends of the earth remember and return to you*
*And all the families of all the nations bow before you*
*For all that is is your domain*
*Your flame kindles all that lives and breathes*
*And you are the motive force of all activity*
*The yearning of the grasses, the lovers' ardor*
*And they that rise up, live, and eat the fat of the earth will*
*    bow before you*
*Before you will bow all those who lie down, find peace, and*
*    enter the dust*
*For none can keep alive by his own power—you alone light*
*    the soul*
*Distant ages to come shall serve you, shall be related to you in*
*    future times*
*Those people not yet born*

*Will sing of your uprightness, your evenness, your brightness*
*To a people not yet born that is still yet to come*
*That this is how you are*

I began writing my own versions of the psalms six years ago, when I was at Gethsemani Abbey and heard the chanting of the psalms in choir. I was really disturbed by the psalms that I heard chanted because they were so violent and passionate. I couldn't imagine how they could be at the center of someone's religious practice. But since I had confidence in the people who were sitting next to me in the choir, I thought I'd better study this matter further. As I got completely involved in the psalms, I came to see and feel how they really go deep in the heart.

### Donald Mitchell

About a month ago, I received a phone call from my mother, who is eighty-six, in the early morning. She had fallen and broken her shoulder, and was about to go to the hospital. The doctors were able to take care of her, and now she is recuperating well.

But when I hung up the telephone that morning, I had all sorts of feelings, mainly fear and worry. As the days passed, I also experienced grief, which surprised me because my mother had not passed away. Then I gradually realized that I was grieving over the eventual loss of my mother. In fact, I understood deep inside that I was already losing her.

How does one deal with these kinds of feelings when facing a loved one's sickness or eventual death? There are certainly many ways of doing so. But I would like to share what I did at the time of my mother's accident because it gives an example of how to live the path of Jesus forsaken. My response is based on the Focolare spirituality, which I practice. So, first I will have to give some background.

As His Holiness Pope John Paul II said in his reflection on the meaning of suffering, we believe that God is love, *agape*. The most powerful self-revelation of this love, we believe, is found in Jesus' self-emptying and self-giving seen when he identified himself on the cross with all suffering humanity. On the cross, Jesus identified himself with each one of us in our sufferings. In my spiritual tradition, this identity of selfless and self-giving love is understood to have reached its peak at the moment that Jesus cried, "My God, my God, why have you forsaken me?" At this holy moment, he had so identified himself with all of us in our suffering—moral, physical, psychological, and spiritual—that he experienced what we find at the very depths of our own suffering: negation, darkness, aloneness, alienation, abandonment.

However, this identity of Jesus with humankind's suffering condition also means that Jesus forsaken brought the presence of God, of God's love, into the depths of our suffering. No matter what our suffering is, or the suffering of others, in it we can find the consoling presence of God. So, in the fear, concern, and grief that I experienced when I received that phone call from my mother, there is also God's loving presence in Jesus forsaken. We can find in our suffering a presence of Jesus forsaken as a doorway to a deeper union with God, to a deeper discovery of God's love for us. And in embracing this presence of Jesus, we also find a pouring forth of his self-emptying, self-giving love that gives us compassionate strength to deal with the cause of our suffering.

So, to be very concrete, when I received that phone call and was facing my troubled feelings inside and my mother's suffering outside, I paused for a moment. In prayer, I went deeply inside this suffering and embraced Jesus forsaken. Finding a deeper union with God, I also found the strength and compassion I needed at that moment to let go of my feelings and go out of myself to care for my mother. But it was not just myself; it was also Christ within me who was loving my mother.

꒰꒱

### Zoketsu Norman Fischer

I think every good teaching has its downside. The downside of the teaching that suffering has redemptive potential is that people can make a virtue of suffering in a way that can be really negative. There is the unsettling fact that sometimes suffering being a path can reinforce and emphasize one's unworthiness with the sense that one should suffer more. And that can be a really unhealthy idea. So the question is, how do you validate the suffering as a path while guarding against that danger?

For example, sometimes women will come to our retreats in Mexico who have for many years been suffering at the hands of husbands who drink too much and beat them up. But through their piety, they have come to believe that it is a virtue to suffer these things and to continue to suffer them. They think: "I become more holy by continuing to endure this suffering." In a way, it is really true, because some do become ennobled by their endurance of suffering. But on the other hand, it doesn't seem to me like a very good idea that they should continue in this way through the valorization of suffering.

### Donald Mitchell

His Holiness Pope John Paul II quotes in his reflection from Paul's letter: "In my flesh I complete what is lacking in Christ's afflictions for the sake of his body, that is the church." In the next paragraph, the pope quotes another passage from Paul: "Now I rejoice in my sufferings for your sake." As the pope goes on to say, the rejoicing comes from the discovery of the redemptive meaning of suffering, that one's suffering is not meaningless. But neither Paul nor the pope is implying that we should seek out suffering, or cling to it.

If suffering comes, we can gain consolation in knowing its deeper meaning in a way that is a real source of comfort and strength. But we cannot stop here. The ministry of Paul and the church has always been one of healing and caring for those in need, and also to seek justice when faced by discrimination or oppression. Finding meaning in our suffering also gives us the strength we need to address what is causing the suffering. God empowers us to address any kind of suffering situation and to seek healing and justice.

On the other hand, there are some who believe that one should bear one's suffering in stoic silence and "offer it up." But this is just bad theology and unhealthy psychology. In my own community, we speak of "Jesus Forsakenitus" as a kind of sickness caused by clinging to suffering, not letting it go so as to pass more fully into the resurrection life. It is not that we just embrace suffering. We embrace Jesus in the suffering and find in him a path of self-giving love to move through the suffering to a deeper participation in the resurrection life of empathy and unity, of communion with God and others in love.

### Father Joseph Wong

I agree that on the cross we find Jesus' deepest sense of alienation and also his most profound transformation. The combination of the two is a mystery. Perhaps here an artist can help us experience it.

I once visited a church in a small town outside the city of Rome called Nemi, by a lake of the same name. Inside the town church, there is an ancient wooden crucifix, a huge one. The peculiar feature of that crucifix is that people can look at it from two different angles. From one angle, you see the agony, the profound suffering and pain of the dying Jesus. But if you go to the other side and look at it from there, then you see the face of Jesus still in the midst of suffering but with perfect calm, serenity, surrender, and peace.

I think the artist did a wonderful job of combining these two aspects in the dying Jesus. It's interesting to note that while Matthew and Mark have only the quotation from the beginning of the Twenty-second Psalm, Luke cites another psalm to bring out the other side of the inner state of Jesus with words of peaceful surrender at the end: "Father, into your hands I commend my spirit" (Psalm 31:5).

Also, if Jesus forsaken is one with the suffering and sin of all humanity, then in commending his spirit to the loving Father, he is also placing all our sins and suffering into God's loving hands. In this mystery of redemption, we can see the mystery of suffering and love.

# CHAPTER SIX

# Love, Compassion, and Communion

### Geshe Lhundub Sopa

Suffering is the subject of the first of the Four Noble Truths in Buddhism. From those four truths, we know that suffering can be relieved temporarily. When we are hungry, we can eat. When we are thirsty, we can drink. When we are hot or cold, we can seek a more comfortable place to be. We can find temporary peace in life, but it is never lasting. Where can we find a lasting peace and happiness, even in the midst of difficult times?

While we always cherish ourselves, we often let that self-cherishing rule our lives in ways that bring suffering rather than happiness to ourselves and others, too. We become self-centered, thinking just of ourselves. We develop an egotistic view of life and a selfish attitude. These in turn are the root of greed, anger, jealousy, anxiety, depression, and so on. What is the antidote in this case? There may be a number of antidotes, but the one that is universal in Buddhism is loving kindness. As we meditate on loving kindness and live it with others, we move our hearts away from an attitude of egoism and its many ills, to an attitude of care and compassion that brings more peace and happiness into our hearts, even in the most difficult of times.

For example, in Buddhism, we talk about the Three Poisons: ignorance, greed, and hatred. Ignorance for us is an egocentric viewpoint, seeing the world from the vantage point of oneself, as a substantial and independent person. From that standpoint, we become attached to things and people through attractions and aversions. Attractions that are self-centered are what we mean by greed. Aversions that are self-centered are what we mean by hate. Greed and hatred, attraction and aversion, become our motivations in life and lead ultimately to unhappiness for ourselves and others. They poison our lives. On the other hand, nongreed, or loving kindness, and nonhate, or compassion, are antidotes to this poison. Love and compassion destroy the roots of our unhappiness. They not only help us let go of greed and hate, but they also help us change our perception of life, our egocentric viewpoint. Without that change in how we see ourselves and the world, our best intentions— even in the religious life—will be compromised.

*Venerable Henepola Gunaratana*

Loving friendliness, or loving kindness, is a very powerful force to transform suffering. We are all born with seeds of loving friendliness, so we all have the capacity to live it. You can find it mentioned everywhere in the Buddha's teachings. We must nurture the seeds of loving friendliness and help them unfold, both in ourselves and in others.

I travel all over the world teaching. One day I was in an airport near London waiting for a flight. I had quite a bit of time, so I was sitting cross-legged on one of the airport benches with my eyes closed practicing loving-friendliness meditation. Then I felt two tiny, tender hands reaching around my neck. I slowly opened my eyes and discovered a very beautiful little toddler. This little one had put her arms around me and was hugging me. I looked over and saw that her mother had come after her. I did not know what language the child spoke, but I said to her in English, "Please go to your mother." The child hung on to my neck and would not let go. Finally the mother carefully snatched her up. But the last I saw of her, she was still struggling to get loose and run back to me.

Maybe because of my robes, this little girl thought I was a Santa Claus or some kind of fairy-tale figure. But at the time I was sitting on that bench, I was sending out thoughts of loving friendliness with every breath. Children are extremely sensitive. When you are angry, they feel those vibrations. When you are full of love and compassion, they feel that, too. This little girl may have been drawn to me by the feelings of loving friendliness she felt.

Under extraordinary circumstances, the power of loving

friendliness breaks through and supersedes every other thought in our minds. Think of the many, many examples of loving friendliness that occurred during the horrible events of September 11, 2001. The firemen who ran up the stairs of the World Trade Center as everyone else was rushing downstairs had but one thought in their minds: saving the lives of others, even though they lost their own. We may not even know we have this quality in ourselves, but the power of loving friendliness is there inside all of us.

Different objects reflect the sun's energy in different ways. In the same way, people differ in their ability to express their loving friendliness. Some people seem naturally warmhearted. Others are more reserved. Perhaps from fear, they are reluctant to open their hearts. Some people struggle to cultivate loving friendliness, others cultivate it without difficulty. According to Buddhist tradition, there is no one who is totally devoid of loving friendliness. It may have been buried under a heap of hatred, anger, and resentment accumulated through a lifetime, perhaps many lifetimes, of unwholesome thoughts and actions. But we can nourish the seeds of loving friendliness until the force of loving friendliness blossoms in all our endeavors.

When we cultivate loving friendliness, we learn to see that others have this kind, gentle nature, however well hidden it might be. Sometimes we have to dig very deep to find it. That is where the effort comes in. Underneath this rough exterior, you may find the jewel that is the person's true nature. The Buddha compared this kind of person to a pond covered by moss. In order to use that water, you must brush the moss aside with your hand.

Our meditation center is in the hills of the West Virginia countryside. When we first opened our center, there was a man down the road who was very unfriendly. I take a long walk every day, and whenever I saw this man, I would wave to him. He would just frown at me and look away. Even so, I would always wave and think kindly of him, sending him loving friendliness. I never gave up on him. After about a year, his behavior changed. He stopped frowning. After another year, as he drove past me he lifted one finger off the steering wheel. Eventually, he took his hand off the steering wheel, stuck it out the window, and waved. Now we are friends.

How can we cultivate our feelings of loving friendliness? We start out by thinking kind thoughts about ourselves. Be full of kindness toward yourself. Accept yourself just as you are. Make peace with your shortcomings. Embrace even your weaknesses. Be gentle and forgiving with yourself as you are at this very moment. If thoughts arise as to how you should be such and such a way, let them go. Let the power of loving friendliness saturate your entire body and mind. Relax in its warmth and radiance.

Once this loving frame of mind is firmly established, think of your loved ones. Next, practice sharing your kind, loving thoughts with all beings. For some people, wishing happiness for a large group of people they do not know may feel forced and difficult, even phony. But remember that this is an exercise in developing your kindness. Every time you think these thoughts, you are strengthening the habit of loving friendliness. In time, your heart grows stronger and the response of loving friendliness becomes automatic.

Finally, we can practice loving friendliness to include our adversaries. This is the category that is the most difficult for most of us. It includes people who have harmed us in some way, our enemies. Even toward these difficult people, we think loving thoughts: "May my adversaries be well, happy, and peaceful. May no harm come to them, may no difficulty come to them."

Practicing loving friendliness can change our habitual negative thought patterns and reinforce positive ones. When we practice loving-friendliness meditation, our minds will become filled with peace and happiness. But loving friendliness is not limited to our thoughts. We must manifest it in our words and our actions.

You can start with the people you have contact with every day. Whenever you see someone, consider that, like yourself, that person wants happiness and wants to avoid suffering. We all feel that way. When we recognize that common ground, we see how closely we are all connected. The woman behind the checkout counter, the man who passes you on the expressway, the young couple walking across the street, the old man in the park feeding the birds. Whenever you see another being, wish for them happiness, peace, and well-being.

Does practicing loving friendliness mean we have to accept everything someone does? Do we let people walk all over us in the name of loving friendliness? If your toddler is headed for a hot stove, you automatically shout at him to stop. Your harsh words are motivated not by anger but by utmost love for the child. Practicing loving friendliness does not mean that we ignore the unwholesome actions of others. It simply means that we respond to such actions in an appropriate way.

But what if someone hurts you? What if someone insults you? You may want to get back at that person. Retaliation is a very human response. But where does that lead? "Hatred is never appeased by more hatred," it says in the *Dhammapada*. An angry response only leads to more anger. If you respond to anger with loving friendliness, the other person's anger will not increase. "By love alone is anger appeased," continue the verses in the *Dhammapada*. So, when someone tries to make you angry or does something to hurt you, stay with your thoughts of loving friendliness toward that person.

With loving friendliness, we recognize more clearly the needs of others and readily help them. We need loving friend-liness in order to live and work with others in harmony. When we cultivate our loving friendliness, we not only make life more pleasant for those around us, our own lives become peaceful and happy.

*Judith Simmer-Brown*
In my work with students, I feel that unrealistic expectations associated with "love" are the cause of incredible suffering. It seems that the word makes loving others sound like it's always easy and joyful. And aspiring to something that has such a pos-

itive expectation for people is often a very difficult leap. I think the problem is that very often we have a lot of snuggly notions about romantic love. Whether in personal relationships or in the spiritual life, we can see love as a kind of magic wand. We just need to wave it and then love will take care of all our problems.

On the other hand, in thinking about young people and the difficulties they face growing up in our materialistic and consumer society, it seems that what they really need is love, acceptance, and encouragement. As a mother of young teenagers and a university teacher who spends hours and hours each week talking to young people, what I hear from them is just wanting someone to be there. Today there are so many "parentless" teenagers in our world who may be given money by their parents but are not given time and attention. The most powerful way to really teach values is to listen with care and affection, in order to help young people come to know and appreciate who they are. This kind of love is not a magic wand but a deep caring that is in the long run profoundly healing.

### Geshe Lhundub Sopa

We have a word in Tibetan for love that means wanting something or someone in order to gain some happiness from possessing that thing or person. So we say, "I love this food," or "I love my job." When we say that we love these things, we expect to gain some kind of happiness from them. We can also speak this way about religious things, like "I love God." "I love my religion." "I love meditation." But is this really love? Often this kind of love involves attachment. We can become attached to food, our job, and even God and our religion. Is there a purer kind of love that is free from this attachment to things and people in order to get more happiness for ourselves?

We have another word for love that means compassion. This kind of love seeks peace and happiness for everyone. It resides deep in our hearts but is often covered over by the other kind of self-seeking love. It is important for a person to distinguish these kinds of love. Then he or she can learn to discern what kind of love is affecting his or her life. The way we can tell is that love with attachment may give us some immediate happiness, but it later fades—often bringing unhappiness. Compassion is a love that brings with it a deeper sense of happiness, a contentment with life that the things we seek and become attached to cannot give us.

꽃

### Abbot John Daido Loori

Love in the positive sense and in the most simplest of terms involves a kind of caring intimacy in which there is difference but not separation. This is what we mean in Buddhism by emptiness.

### Brother Paul Quenon

The mystic John the Cross made a supreme effort to distinguish between attachment and love. In his sense of these terms, love requires detachment, and therefore it's a kind of emptiness. You don't love the other person for your own sake, or for some gratification that you get, but you love the person for his or her sake. There is humility in this, for you yourself have to have an emptiness on your own part to be able to love. In this self-emptying love, there is difference between people but the separation between them is dissolved into a deep loving unity of communion.

### Father Thomas Ryan

Relationships provide us with the skillful means to grind and polish each other until we are diamonds with facets that sparkle with love. I am a celibate priest, but I strongly believe that family life is a more radical asceticism for true holiness. The universal Christian vocation is availability for service in love. When I see parents raising a family of children, I observe a radical availability for service in love on the part of the parents. So I recognize family life as one of the genuine ways to holiness. Its counterpart in religious orders and congregations is community life, which is precisely the skillful means from which our spiritual life proceeds. Family life and community life provide the grinding and sanding, the diminishment of our egos, the possibility for growth in love and communion that lead to holiness.

⚜

### Prioress Mary Collins

One of the great paradoxes of Benedictine life is that community living does not protect monastics from the suffering humans cause themselves and one another. When newcomers to my community are smarting from the conflicts that appear in human interaction, I tell them that we need to think of ourselves as thrown together in the tumbler of community, where we bump into one another repeatedly and begin to break through one another's defenses and reach into the concealed places of our hearts. Our monasteries, despite our idealism, our aspirations, and our rhetoric about peace and harmony, are not really completely violence-free zones.

But while we find ourselves being polished and also abraded by the interactions among us, it is also true that the members of the community, through this interaction and the suffering we cause one another, find their way through the suffering. The way we do this is through a genuine ability to reach out to others in love. There is a passage in the Benedictine *Rule* in which Benedict talks about never turning away from someone who needs your love. This is in fact the practice that is most prominent in my community. We may be the source of suffering to one another, but it is also true that our interrelationships mediate and develop love between us.

There is a lesson here for everyone. In a marriage, or any lasting relationship, you can also find this kind of suffering interaction. You can begin to feel that you are stuck with each other, like we are in the monastery. But see in this situation the opportunity for growth in love, the discovery of the true meaning of love.

There is a memory I have of an elderly sister who came to one of our community meetings. She was up in her nineties and had never spoken to the community at any chapter meeting, much less go right up to a microphone. She had been born in Germany and still spoke with a heavy German accent. There we were at this meeting, trying to decide what we were going to do about something or other, and there was definitely some contention in the voices and in the interaction of ideas. To our surprise, this elderly woman got up, worked her way to the microphone, looked out at the community, and said to all of us, "Sisters, God loves us. That love is *the* reality!"

That, of course, was the truth of her life, and it was the truth of the community's life. It was interesting to see how our hearing of it from her shifted the discussion to a whole different tone.

When Benedict is talking about the fourth step of humility in his *Rule,* he observes that the monastic who is growing in humility is able to endure the difficulties that come from having to live under unfavorable or even unjust conditions. He says that the one who is developing a monastic heart is able quietly to embrace that suffering, even enduring it without weakening or seeking escape.

This sounds almost magical, but I would like to insist that the theology underlying it is the theology that I see embodied in the community. The theology of the cross gives us a deep awareness of the pain and suffering that we see in one another—whether it's suffering we bring on ourselves by our own negativity, or suffering that we cause one another, or suffering that a sister undergoes because of a very difficult situation even before she ever came to community. We see in the suffering something to be honestly recognized and responded to by going out of ourselves to the suffering person in love.

This is the mystery that is operating in the community; I call it the mystery of embodiment. It manifests itself in the fact that the sisters, having internalized the mystery of Christ's suffering as well as the mystery of Christ's compassion, do go directly out to one another when there is pain. Since we are a large community, there is always someone whose spiritual maturity is such that she has the wisdom to see who is suffering and reach out to that person.

How, then, can people who find themselves interacting in troubling ways and causing one another suffering actually find hope for relief from such suffering? The answer is to be found in the assurance to us of Christ's love and in Benedict's charge to us: "Never turn away when someone needs your love."

I would add that it is very often those who are least among us—those who are not prominent leaders in the community, those who are perhaps not the best educated, those whose egos are small but whose compassion is great—who are the ones able to reach out and make the needed gesture of love. This is in fact the path of the cross, the way of unconditional love, for it is offered to everyone no matter what the suffering is and without regard for whether the person brought it on herself or whether it is from something that has preceded her. There is profound healing in this path of suffering transformed into love.

### Sister Mary Margaret Funk

The kind of transformation of suffering into love is accomplished through God's mercy, and it's through mercy that we experience genuine humility. Let me give an example from my own community about a nun who recently died. Her name is Sister Mary Gerald, and she had retired from working at our St. Paul Hermitage, which is a facility for about 115 elderly residents. There she had been the supervisor of the kitchen, and had twenty-five workers who reported to her. She had been there for twenty-six years and was a very, very gifted cook.

Now, I was the prioress when Sister Mary Gerald retired and returned to the monastery. So, I had the happy opportunity of assigning her to the monastery kitchen. Well, in the monastic kitchen, she reported to a woman younger than herself and with a reading disability, another woman who had multiple handicaps—hearing, sight, and probably cooking wasn't her strength—and another cook who had practically no experience at all.

Sister Mary Gerald and I would meet once a month to talk about how things were going, and she reported real inadequacies in the food preparation, cleanliness, nutrition, presentation, purchasing, and so on. In short, nothing in the monastery kitchen was up to Mary Gerald's standards and experience, her "former way of life," as we put it.

Then one day I was walking out of church and was on my way to my office when she came right up beside me and said, "I got it! I got it!" I replied, "Well, what did you get?" She again said, "I got it!" And then, speaking softer and softer, she said, "I got that the kitchen is not about food. It's about love."

### Father James Wiseman

As I reflect on the story of Sister Mary Gerald, it seems to me that she had a genuine conversion. She stopped regarding her superiors in the new kitchen as people totally separate from herself. Instead, in more traditional Christian language, she saw that she was now one with them in Christ, called to love them as she loved herself. This is the kind of love that wants and seeks the best for the other person. It doesn't mean that the food no longer mattered, but it wasn't the main dish being served in the kitchen. It was getting priorities right. It was about the way she was now going to treat other people.

This story also points us to what is ultimate: communion rather than separate individuality. One thing that monastic life can show everyone is that you are not alone in the world, there is a deeper unity to life that is discovered in love. This loving unity shows us that ultimate reality is the beauty of living together in communion. In this communion, we find our true selves and our true happiness.

Benedict's *Rule* gives guidelines for developing this communion. In its next-to-last chapter, there is the beautiful phrase that the monks are to vie with one another in obedience. This is not about giving directions right and left that others have to obey. It means trying to be alert to what others' needs are rather than always seeking to satisfy your own. Another beautiful passage of the Benedictine *Rule* speaks of the abbot's charge to see that the sick are especially cared for. And elsewhere in the *Rule,* Benedict speaks of the young and the very elderly as those who need special attention. These guidelines represent attitudes and practices that are helpful for all people who want to grow in love and live in communion.

### Father Damon Geiger

I would like to offer an Eastern Christian perspective on our communal relationship to the rest of creation. Since we believe that every human being assumes the whole creation in himself or herself in the sense that we are a microcosm of all creation, then our salvation is tied up with the salvation of the world. We are not to be saved *from* the world, but we can only be saved *with* the world.

Moreover, Scripture tells us that we humans were given the responsibility to be stewards of the creation, not owners. Creation does not belong to any of us, but to God; we are only to cultivate and till it. As stewards, we must render accounts to one another and to God for our stewardship, administering the rest of creation according to the owner's intent, which is that of communion. If we do properly administer the creation, then the whole creation becomes a sacrament of communion.

How many sacraments do we have? Well, as Easterners, we say at least seven, since the ideal is that everything is a sacrament and as such is to be administered according to the will of the owner, which is to bring about communion with him and with one another.

The terrible thing about the Fall is that we've turned the creation from being a sacrament into being a sacrilege, a sacrilege that has become a curse. The meaning of Christ's redemption is that he assumed the whole of the creation, even as he assumed our human nature, and, in so doing, he resacramentalized it. We are called to rediscover this sacramentality of all things, allowing them to become a source of communion. This includes seeing each other as fellow stewards, not as rivals or competitors to be used or manipulated. A lot of work remains to be done here.

### Father Donald Grabner

As a footnote, I would add that original sin is one of the most badly understood teachings in Christianity today. Original sin is not an actual sin, not a personal sin. The individual is not guilty of original sin. Genesis tell us that human nature is good, indeed very good. Yet we all have a tendency, a temptation to evil. So, while we are essentially good, we have this tendency toward evil. We have both original goodness and original sin. As in Buddhism, there is original perfection or awakening and the tendency toward evil and suffering. How we recognize this tendency as present in us without losing our sense of worth and dignity is one of the big issues in the spiritual life.

### Ajahn Amaro

In Christianity, since God is love and unity, loving communion between persons can be considered a living out of Ultimate Reality. For Buddhists, community is also a deeply significant center of our lives. In one very well-known teaching of the Buddha, Ananda, who was the Buddha's attendant and frequently the fall guy of many Buddhist dialogues, says, "I think that spiritual friendship is half of the holy life." When Ananda asks the Buddha about this, the Buddha replies, "Not so, Ananda. It is not half of the holy life. It's the whole of the holy life."

What is spiritual friendship? The Buddha says it is not only having noble spiritual companions and harmonious relationships with them. It is also friendship with the "lovely," with the good or the beautiful. This means that there is an internal relation of the heart with goodness and beauty that one discovers in a spiritual friendship. And externally this goodness and beauty one finds in a spiritual relation manifests as unity or harmony in unselfish and compassionate relationships with other beings. The growth of this goodness and beauty in the compassionate heart and in our relationships purifies our tendencies toward the kinds of unwholesome thoughts, words, and actions that alienate us from others and block our, and their, happiness.

# CHAPTER SEVEN

# *Emotional Healing*

## FROM A SENSE OF UNWORTHINESS
## TO SELF-ACCEPTANCE

*Ajahn Sundara*

To find love and unity with others, there is often a great deal of emotional healing that needs to take place. However, the whole realm of emotions and feelings is experienced as a rather messy one. Anyone who meditates knows that dealing with thoughts, watching them come and go, is not so difficult. Dealing with body sensation is also not that difficult. But emotions are another story. They are sticky, confusing, bewildering, and can appear very permanent. They test our patience to the limit.

In working with emotions, it seems that the feeling of fear is very much part of the mess. It is very easy to talk about our fears, but when we probe them, we find that it is a very long process to get down to the actual pain associated with them. We all want to be free from fear, but the pain behind it is hard to face. The painfulness of our fears impels us to turn our attention away, outside of ourselves, and blame or attack what we fear or who threaten us. We need to work with these emotions both within ourselves and in our relationships.

Our community, composed of monks and nuns living as one community and adjusting to an Asian hierarchical and patriarchal monastic form, has found that there are many and sometimes subtle ways to do violence to one another. It is often done unconsciously out of fear of losing control, power, and status. As we gradually became aware of the need to learn to relate to each other healthily, we entered a period of regular meetings and open dialogues. These have helped us to understand the dynamic involved in relating with men and women committed to the monastic life, to become conscious, at a deeper level, of our conditioning in relationship with one another and to address gender issues.

After nearly fifteen years, the community of both monks and nuns has learned to respect and appreciate this process as well as the challenges inherent in it. I might add that part of that resolution was to recognize and accept the fundamental difference between men and women. This kind of process, of dialogue, is important to all persons both for emotional health and healthy relationships.

### Father Thomas Keating

The root of both personal unhappiness and social unrest, it seems to me, is found in what might be called the false-self system. The Christian tradition presents various events in the life of Christ as manifesting the divine intention for the healing transformation of the human family. One such event was when Jesus, after being baptized in the Jordan, went into the desert under the influence of the Spirit. There he experienced the three basic instinctual needs that are the source of all our emotional and social difficulties, namely, the needs of security and survival, approval and affection, and power and control.

These, of course, are the instincts that an infant needs in order to survive, but we are supposed to move beyond these as centers of motivation as we proceed through childhood, adolescence, and on into adult life. Unfortunately, by about the age of four, these instinctual needs begin to fossilize into programs for emotional happiness, so that happiness is felt to lie in the instant gratification of one or another of these needs.

It's in the desert that we confront the dark side of our own personality and begin to be awakened to the damage that the instinctual needs for happiness without any moderating influences are causing us. Given our particular temperament, we tend to fossilize our desires for happiness in a certain direction; and the false self begins to be formed. This might be called the "homemade self," that is, the self made in our own image rather than in the image of God, in which the Judeo-Christian tradition believes we were originally created.

So, here we are at four years of age with programs for happiness that identify with the symbols in our culture that respect security, power, and esteem ideals. When these are frustrated, as they usually are, and even all day long for some people, off go the afflictive emotions: shame, humiliation, grief, discouragement, depression, anxiety, fear, and anger. These afflictive emotions can become so painful that we repress them into the unconscious, where the energy remains opposing the free flow of the natural energies and the energy of grace. This is what in St. Paul's language is called "the old man" in each of us.

The false self is just a contemporary term for that process, and it basically manifests itself in three major consequences: illusion as to what true happiness is, craving to find happiness in the wrong places, and weakness of will, which means that even if we find out where true happiness is to be found, we are too weak to do anything about it anyway. Obviously this is a rather dim view of human nature, to say the least, but it happens to be the truth according to Revelation.

Hence arises the need for redemption, which is not an issue about getting to heaven at the last minute but is an issue of God's intent to radically heal us at the very roots of where our problems all began. These roots are found in the emotional programs for happiness that still manifest themselves in negative tendencies in daily life which, in turn, secretly influence our decisions, and indeed do so all through life unless we embark on the spiritual journey.

All of us have a great deal of these issues rumbling around inside our unconscious and manifesting in daily life. You won't have to look very hard around the world today to realize that when these tendencies have free rein and a whole bunch of false selves turn up in the same place or in the same ethnic group, nation, or religion, then there is going to be a terrible mess.

Religion, with all its idealism, has been the worst of all organizations in the history of the world as far as violence is concerned. How could that be? Given the calls to peace, unity, and all the things we normally hear on Sundays and holy days, what happened? Evidently, so many of our Christian people have never heard the Gospel at a deep enough level to understand what it really means. Look at Rwanda: 90 percent Christian, 80 percent Catholic, and they just tore each other to pieces with their machetes. Had they never heard of the Gospel? Apparently it had no effect on them.

This is the root problem: We put too much energy into programs for happiness that can't possibly work in adult life. Instead of evaluating what our basic motivation is as we become adults, instead of doing something effective about our emotional programs, we think up bigger and better ways of doing the same stupid things: better ways of getting more security, more approval, more power and control. And so it goes on and on.

The other world religions have the same basic insight as Christianity into this illness of the human condition that is rooted in the false self. All forms of therapy that don't eventually confront this issue will only produce further disease. The greatest of all the tricks of the false self is an addiction. This is a way of preoccupying ourselves so much with our emotional programs of security, control, and approval that we really never have to feel the pain of their inevitable frustration. For it's feeling the pain that leads to the healing of emotional diseases—not acting it out, not repressing it into the unconscious, and not creating some compensatory way of avoiding it.

When the "I" becomes the center of the universe around which all our faculties and all our experiences circulate like planets around the sun, anything entering our gravitational field is judged not on the basis of its reality but on how well it suits our need for more power, approval, or security. And this is basically the human condition, its original sin as it were, as Jesus addresses it in the Gospel and from which he invites us to graduate.

The divine therapy that Jesus offers as a cure for this illness is initiated in what he calls our "inner room" in Matthew 6:6. If we follow the suggestion to enter our inner room, where is it to be found? It's not on the psychological level of our consciousness. It's rather at the spiritual level of our being, the level of intuition and the spiritual will. This therapeutic process turns us toward the center of our being, where the divine presence, according to Christian faith, is waiting for us, has waited for us, and is always available twenty-four hours a day our whole life long.

That divine indwelling is the root and fundamental principle on which the Christian spiritual journey is based. It's the presence of God, intensifying through love until it penetrates the whole of our being at every level. This is the spiritual marriage—the transformation of our false-self motivation to the values of the Gospel, of faith, hope, and love.

The next question is: What goes on in the inner room, if you agree to go there? The first work of the divine therapy is to affirm our basic goodness as creatures made in the image of God. This suggests that along with our psychological unconscious, which is the place where we repress emotionally unbearable trauma, there exists equally and more important the ontological unconscious. This is the level of the divine indwelling itself, the presence in us of the Father, Son, and Holy Spirit, the Divine Trinity, the source of all reality. This creative presence is always in us; hence the impossibility for God ever to be absent from us.

So, if we exist, then it means that God always dwells within us at a deep level and is trying by every possible means to awaken us to that presence. It's this presence that is transforming, divinizing, and liberating, healing the emotional wounds of early life.

What is the significance of this healing process in our struggle with suffering? Perhaps it means that when we feel the pain of the emptiness of the false self, when we experience the dark nights, when our ideas of God, Christ, and church are shattered, at that moment our redemption in the fullest sense takes place. In this open place, we identify with Christ as he has first identified with us, and it is not a disaster but a door into the fullness of inner resurrection.

Perhaps there is a deeper reality even than this, namely that suffering and death are the resurrection. This is suggested in the Gospel of John, where Jesus is depicted as reigning from the Cross. In other words, the diversity and unity of God manifest in the crucifixion of Christ have become unified, so that the very moment of Christ's death and the very pain that accompanies it are perceived to be resurrection itself. In other words, God is in all, as St. Paul says, and Christ is everything in everyone. If we look at suffering and transformation from this Christian perspective, the passion and resurrection are so closely united that pain is joy, and joy is pain, and God is in both and beyond both.

### Zenkei Blanche Hartman

In the Mahayana tradition, we daily chant the bodhisattva vows, the vows of one who aspires to awaken to reality, to our True Self, for the benefit of all beings.

> *Beings are numberless. I vow to free them or to awaken*
> *with them.*
> *Delusions are inexhaustible. I vow to cut through them.*
> *Dharma gates are boundless. I vow to enter them.*
> *Buddha's way is unsurpassable. I vow to become it.*

At the same time, we recognize our limitations, our incompleteness, our false self. We are faced with the many wounds from our past. So our repentance is also endless. We live a life of vow and repentance, constant joyful effort and constant falling short.

Somehow we humans seem to have lost our awareness of our interdependence and connectedness with all that is. As a result, we've fallen into the basic ignorance that is at the heart of all suffering: the belief that we are separate, isolated entities. Then add to this sense of separateness an early conditioning that may have fixed notions of unworthiness, something wrong, not good enough, unacceptable, in our minds.

Where do these feelings of unworthiness come from? Ordinarily in the process of socialization, adults, with no malevolent intent, say things like "Don't do that!" "Put that down!" "Don't you ever listen!" "Shame on you!" This process burdens us with a false self and further blinds us to our fundamental interrelatedness with others in which we find our True Self. In fact, our sense of unworthiness can make us feel alienated from others. It can be an especially heavy burden that a person feels he or she carries alone.

But when someone steps into our Zen Center, perhaps without even having heard the words "taking refuge," they may have the direct experience of being welcomed just as they are. At least that is our effort and our intention, based on the example of Suzuki Roshi. However, once free of an oppressive structure, which created a lifelong sense of unworthiness, some people find that the new freedom releases an urge to assert that self that was so long denied. The precepts and guidelines for practice governing a person's conduct in the community may be opposed or resisted as restrictions on their new sense of personal freedom.

Eventually, the discipline of daily *zazen* meditation, bowing, chanting *sutras,* communal work, following the schedule, interaction with fellow monks, and regular discussions with the teacher may enable monastics to experience the underlying reality of the precepts: that their origin is not outside but within themselves. They are expressions of how we really want to live so as not to cause harm and are not demands placed on people by some outside authority.

How do teachings in Buddhism address feelings of unworthiness and alienation? First, in those teachings there are many references to our original wholeness. The ordination ceremony begins with the statement "In faith that we are Buddha, we enter Buddha's way." In the very first Dharma talk, or formal teaching, I heard, Suzuki Roshi said, "You are perfect just as you are." He said other things like: "You have everything you need." "You are already complete." "Just to be alive is enough." In my case, I knew I couldn't be the sole exception to all these assertions, and it became my *koan* to try to understand what he was talking about.

I found that many of the old teaching stories of Zen have a similar tone. For example:

*Ta-mei asked Ma-tsu, "What is Buddha?"*
*Ma-tsu said, "This very mind is Buddha."*

Also, the primary teaching of the *Lotus Sutra* is that the fundamental nature of all living beings is Buddha-nature, the nature of awakening. Throughout that Scripture is the assurance that every being will be a Buddha some day. And according to the *Flower Ornament Sutra,* when the Buddha was enlightened, he said, "I now see that all sentient beings everywhere fully possess the wisdom and virtues of the enlightened ones. But because of false conceptions and attachments, they don't realize it."

This is just a sampling of teachings pointing at our original perfection. And the last one calls our attention to the false conceptions about our self and the attachments that hinder our realization of our True Self. Here is where our daily practice, study, and regular interactions with our fellow monastics and our teacher can help us to see more clearly. But even with all these teachings, the examples of teachers and daily practice, how is it that the sense of personal unworthiness can persist?

In my own experience, I found it still potent when I was invited to serve as abbess after twenty-seven years of practice. I decided that I could not accept the invitation without first getting to the root of my need for acceptance from outside. I had to find what I thought was unacceptable about me. So I did some work with a friend, who was both a therapist and a Zen practitioner. With her help, I was finally able to fully embrace that whiny three-year-old girl who didn't want to be the boy she was expected to be. I was able to accept myself as the particular female I am, which I had always rejected even as I had been a militant feminist.

The other thing I found out in that therapy was that as long as I could remember, I had the assumption that I needed to do something good in the world in order to deserve to be alive. I had been caught by the conceit that I can and should save the world in one fashion or another all my adult life, and also knew the matching despair that I can't. As for doing good, I now realize that since we all possess the wisdom and compassion of the awakened ones, naturally we want to do good and not cause harm. It's not a matter of the intention of our will but of the nature of our life. All we need to do to deserve to be alive is to accept the gift of this life.

There are several aspects of our monastic life that may cause us to question our conditioned notion that we are unworthy. For example, it is our custom to stop, put our hands palm to palm, and bow as we pass one another in walking along a path, or down a corridor, or whenever we may meet. When we serve food, server and served bow to each other, and we all take turns serving and being served. Having this experience of bowing and being bowed to constantly reinforces the teaching that all are worthy of respect.

Our ceremonial life also addresses the judgment of oneself as unworthy. Pretty much everything we do—sitting *zazen,* eating, bowing, chanting, *dokusan* (private interview with the abbot), walking meditation—all are done in an erect, dignified posture. Our posture and deportment training insists on an erect as opposed to a slouching posture. A slouching posture often reflects a mind that judges itself as unworthy. If the slouching becomes a habit, often the person will feel unworthy all the time without being aware of it.

My experience of Suzuki Roshi was of someone who totally respected everyone, who saw Buddha in everyone. Meeting in private interview, he invariably held everyone in positive regard. It has been my aspiration ever since to cultivate that possibility in myself. Alas, I often fall short. But I truly believe that this is the most potent transformative aspect of monastic practice. If the abbess or abbot can see Buddha in everyone and demonstrates it in actions of body, speech, and mind, the monastics will learn from that example.

Finally, let me mention one person who successfully did learn from Suzuki Roshi's example. Tommy Dorsey was a transvestite entertainer and heroin addict. He joined our Zen Center and went on to be abbot of a Zen temple in the Castro District, the gay area of San Francisco. Tommy experienced much personal suffering as well as the unconditional love of Suzuki Roshi. This love enabled Tommy to become a source of love and compassion for all of us who knew him. During the worst part of the AIDS epidemic, when there was little treatment yet available, he founded an AIDS hospice adjoining his Zen temple. He personally cared for many of the early AIDS patients.

Suzuki Roshi also added to "You are perfect just as you are" the words "There is always room for improvement." This has also been an enormously encouraging paradox! My deepest aspiration, and I cannot do it but keep trying, is to accept myself as I am and at the same time make my best effort in each present moment. What else can we do?

### Father James Wiseman

Like most of you, in my lifetime I've witnessed all kinds of suffering, sometimes very severe kinds. I was once awakened in the middle of the night to go help someone who was in such excruciating physical pain that all he could do was scream and howl as I tried frantically to get an ambulance to take him to the hospital. Another time I was called out in the middle of the night to go to someone already in the hospital, facing imminent death and terrified at the thought. I could go on and on, but of all of the kinds of suffering I've witnessed, I think the saddest was something that was once said in a very matter-of-fact, even depressed tone of voice: "I feel that I'm no damn good."

As you know, that's an attitude that's very prevalent, especially among young people today. It's something that can indeed lead to suicide; and statistics show that among teenagers, suicide is one of the leading causes of death in this country.

Well, to return to the person who said "I feel I'm no damn good," what's the root of this? The person who said that is in fact a wonderful person, very much loved by those who know him. So the roots of his sense of unworthiness may come from his childhood, how he was treated or not treated by loved ones. But the way this negative false–self image was being played out today could be seen in his comparing himself with others and noticing only that he didn't have their gifts. These gifted people became the standard against which he compared himself, and he concluded that he always fell short. In other words, he was apparently in the grip of what John Cassian many centuries ago would have called the thought of envy.

Both in his *Institutes* and in his *Conferences,* Cassian has some very penetrating reflections on the basic unhealthy thoughts we all have: pride, vainglory, gluttony, lust, anger, dejection, sloth, and envy. Although we often hear that pride is the root of all evil, Cassian makes a very interesting remark. He says that in some ways envy is even worse because of the way it is directed against God. It's a sense of regret at seeing the gifts that God has given someone else and wishing they were your own. It is not accepting yourself the way God made you.

There is perhaps no easy corrective to envy or the lack of self-acceptance. But surely one thing that may help is to recognize that what really matters is not being a separate individual but a member of a community. We find our true self not in competition with others but in communion with others. We speak of this unity in Christian terms as the whole Christ, the body of Christ, head and members.

A wonderful insight is given into this reality by St. Thérèse of Lisieux, who was recently named a doctor of the church, a title that means a kind of official teacher. Therese recognized that she was not some brilliant intellectual. She hadn't even finished secondary school. But she also recognized the beauty of this notion of the full body of Christ in all of its variety, with all of the different gifts that St. Paul talks about. To illustrate this point, she used the marvelous image of a field of flowers, pointing out how boring and monotonous it would be if the only flowers in the world were the lilies and roses, the kind of glorious blossoms we put before religious statues. She noted that in fact God delights just as much in the small violets and wildflowers along the side of the road; all are of equal value as parts of the total variety.

If we could really live out this teaching by recognizing that each one of us, just as we are, is already complete and of great value, we could cultivate our own gifts and rejoice in those of others. Our value is ingrained and does not depend on who we are or what we do. If we will recognize humbly and truthfully that no one can be all things to all people, then I think we avoid that terrible sense of unworthiness that can lead a person to say "I'm no damn good."

꙳

## Joseph Goldstein

The impulse toward unworthiness has many voices in our minds. There are the voices of "I'm not good enough." "I can't do this." "Did I do something wrong?" It's the feeling that somehow we don't quite measure up. In Buddhism this tendency toward comparing oneself with others—and the comparison can be either I'm better than, I'm worse than, I'm equal to—is called conceit. It's that pattern of comparing.

This conditioning of conceit—I'm better than, I'm equal to, I'm worse than—is said not to be uprooted from our minds until the final stage of awakening. We can have uprooted pride, uprooted desire, uprooted anger and ill will, and still this pattern of conceit keeps arising within us. So it's very powerful. It's very deeply conditioned. And because it is so strong and so deep, it feels like we need to understand it carefully, to really investigate how it's working.

Feelings of unworthiness through comparison arise from

many causes, many social conditions: our parents, schools, friends, society, and so on. Think of the comparing mind that is conditioned by advertising. How could we not feel somehow inadequate when we continually see all these beautiful, happy, smiling, contented, perfect people? This is what's being fed to us, and we measure ourselves against these images. We develop a self-concept against these images and then feel bad about ourselves.

However, even when we see through the ruse of social conditioning, feelings of unworthiness still affect us when we come face-to-face with our own hearts and minds. It arises not only in comparison to what's out there; it also comes when we look inside. In this regard, psychology can help us understand our background, our present environment, and our own emotional predispositions that may be feeding our feelings of unworthiness. Therapy can be a good tool for untangling this often-complex web of personal history. Shedding light on the particular issues of our relationships can weaken the glue of unwholesome patterns.

On a more fundamental level, as Buddhists we see feelings of unworthiness as also rooted in what the Buddha called wrong views, a set of misconceptions that create a false understanding of the world and ourselves. Someone once said to the Dalai Lama, "I do not feel worthwhile as a person." The Dalai Lama replied forcefully, "Your feeling of having no value is wrong. Absolutely wrong. You are deceiving yourself." In other words, the problem is not with *being* unworthy, the problem is with the *feeling* of unworthiness. If we *feel* unworthy, we often conclude that we *are* unworthy, which is a wrong view. Recognizing this false view is a step in changing how we feel about ourselves.

When I first went to Asia in 1967 and was practicing in Bodhgaya, India, I was just starting to learn meditation. I would sit and I would see all the judgments, fears, and desires in my mind. I would then go running to my teacher, telling him what a terrible person I was. It was really my first deep and careful look into my own mind. And, of course, my teacher would just smile and say, "Just go back and watch your breath and be mindful." I would go back and see more of this stuff.

This was the beginning of an insight that has stayed with me all these years: "If it's not one thing, it's another." There is always something coming up that we have to deal with. There is a line from *Zorba the Greek* where he says, "Self-knowledge is always bad news."

Anyone on a contemplative journey, looking into oneself, into one's heart and mind, will see that, and it is not simply a question of these negative or unwholesome thoughts and feelings. It is also seeing the unskillful actions we take. It's not only limited to what's within us; it's how we are acting in the world. It includes the patterns of unwholesome behavior we live based on these feelings of unworthiness.

An incident that happened almost twenty years ago was a transforming moment for me in my spiritual journey. My teacher at the time was very demanding, fierce even—like an old Zen master. One time I was giving a report on my experience, and he looked at me and said, "That's not true." My heart sank because at that moment I realized that he was right. I was shading my experience because I wanted to move it along more quickly. I realized that my behavior was shameful, and I spent days with feelings of unworthiness, remorse, regret, and guilt.

But then something happened. After days of being immersed in those feelings, a light began to emerge. And that was the recognition that acceptance of our shadow side is the key. As soon as I could admit to myself that in fact I could shade the truth, I could lie even in a situation where I never thought I would, in the moment when I opened to that possibility, there was a tremendous sense of relief. The relief came because I was coming into balance with what was true rather than sustaining the inner pressure of keeping that shadow side of me away from myself.

I think that this is a very important turning point in our spiritual journeys. For me, it was very significant when I realized I would much rather see my defilements, sins, unwholesome tendencies—whatever words we use to describe those negative forces—than not see them. That was revelatory for me, because it opened up the possibility of seeing the totality of myself without self-judgment and without comparison.

Carl Jung said, "One does not become enlightened by imagining figures of light, but by making the darkness conscious. The latter procedure, however, is disagreeable and therefore not popular." It is disagreeable at first. But what has been so amazing over all these years is that I think we come to a point where our commitment to the truth is so strong that actually there's a feeling of delight in seeing the flaws, in seeing defilements. Now, when I watch my mind, I'm so happy to see them because in the seeing of them is the possibility of being free to make choices that are guided more by loving kindness and compassion.

In Theravada Buddhism, we have something that is perhaps similar to baptism. We call it "entering the stream." In entering the stream there is the first genuine authentic realization of selflessness, of going beyond this notion of ego self. When we have this authentic baptism into selflessness, into the emptiness of self, then we see that unworthiness is not the problem. What is a problem is our identification with that feeling. We realize that while we may sometimes *feel* unworthy, which will happen until we are fully awakened beings, we *are not* unworthy. And when we develop the wisdom to see the insubstantiality of our feelings, then they become simply arisings in the mind. We don't condemn ourselves for having them, and we do not necessarily act on them, either. In this way, the feelings of unworthiness lose their self-lacerating power.

"Easier said than done," one might reply. Here are some suggestions from our tradition that might be helpful in deconditioning patterns of unworthiness. Recognize the feeling. Accurately label it. Then accept the emotion for what it is, and don't wallow in it or justify it. A useful mantra is: "It's okay. Let me feel it." Finally, ask yourself how you are getting hooked by the feeling. The purpose of this question is not so much to find an answer but to change the locus of observation. When we ask about a feeling, we shift away from being caught in it. We need to remember that all emotions are just that, emotions. They come and go. The feeling of unworthiness is an emotion that comes and goes due to certain causes, just like all other feelings. We don't have to drown in it thinking that we are actually unworthy. Like all emotions, it is workable—we need not be enslaved by it into believing a wrong view about ourselves.

### Father James Wiseman

When we recognize a painful truth about ourselves, we feel terrible. But when we recognize the truth, accept it, and admit it, it can be freeing. I would just like to give a couple of examples of this, one positive and one negative. I myself think that among the most remarkable and praiseworthy things Pope John Paul II has done, especially in the years leading up to the celebration of the new millennium, was frankly and truthfully to admit and ask pardon for the wrongs that have been done by the church over the centuries. There is even a book out entitled *When a Pope Asks Forgiveness.* This was a remarkable and a very freeing thing for the church.

Negatively—and I don't say this to sound unduly critical of a particular person—I think a lot of the problems that Cardinal Law has brought on himself in the Archdiocese of Boston are due to his not forthrightly recognizing the evil that had been occurring in his diocese and his contributing to this by just moving sexually abusive priests to other parishes. On both a personal level and an institutional level, it's only the truth that can make us free.

*Stephanie Kaza*

One of my own personal experiences of feeling tremendously inadequate and unworthy was sometime in the early 1980s. I was quite ill at the time, and the advice I received from one of my coworkers was: "Try just to be a really good animal right now. Go out and lie on the beach, be warm, get the right food and drink."

From an animal's perspective, being inadequate is a very real concern. If you don't get enough food, or shelter, or you can't run fast enough from a predator, there are serious consequences. So it's good to recognize your inadequacies in order to compensate in some way. It's not bad to be inadequate; it's just part of living an animal existence.

Whether it's coming from a Christian or a Buddhist perspective, I stumble the most when the judgmental, dualistic mind adds *unworthiness* on top of *inadequacy*. It's this dualism of good/bad that weighs me down, not the actual inadequacy. It has been important to realize that having inadequacies does not make me unworthy. Inadequacy is a fact of life; unworthiness is the added burden we construct for ourselves. A healthy humility would be a kind of surrender to the animal existence that is at the core of who we are as living beings. That is a beautiful thing, not a terrible thing. It is a gorgeously evolved capacity to understand the subtlety of need and drive.

### Sister Mary Margaret Funk

The greatest source of dejection that I experience is what could be called down thoughts, which when unchecked lead to a very harsh, dark, damp funk. We add these kinds of thoughts onto the problems we face in daily life. I may bump into one of my inadequacies, my habitual failings, and then add thoughts like: "I never get it right." "I will always feel this way." "She is right, I am a loser."

The classic spiritual teaching for dealing with such added-on thoughts is that just as one is to refrain from putting one-self "up" in vainglory, one should refrain from putting oneself "down" in dejection. I am to give God the glory when praised, and when blamed, I am not to let the words of others affect my core being. I am to accept the truth about myself "as I am" with humility, knowing that the truth will set me free.

Like any human, I can expect to be harmed, misunderstood, humiliated, and disregarded. I can also expect to be bothered by shortcomings, inadequacies, weaknesses, and limitations. Being human has nothing to do with entitlements or perfections. Patiently suffering through the difficult times brought on by others or ourselves is the fully human way. Most of the time a sense of unworthiness is just "a thought" that simply comes and goes if I do not nurture it or make it swollen with extra commentary. I am not my thoughts about myself.

This kind of ascetical practice of letting go of our negative thoughts about ourselves brings with it the grace to make the changes necessary, to love others and to be loving toward ourselves. I must avoid harsh thinking about myself, since this creates unstable and reactive patterns that keep me from praying and from being an attentive listener to my sisters; it also blocks my ability to give them good counsel. Dejected thoughts are self-violent tactics that also prepare my mind to express hostility toward others. Loving myself renders me more loving toward others. There is a close link between the way I think about myself and the way I regard others.

### Reverend Shohaku Okumura

The teacher of my teacher said, "*Zazen* is good for nothing. The more I sit, the more I see I'm no good." At the beginning of my practice, this was very important to me. As I struggled, his words gave me comfort. As I progress, they are still important. The sense that I am unworthy is very precious to me. It is not self-deprecating but a realistic acceptance of weaknesses and limitations. There is a kind of wisdom in it. It keeps me humble, free from a sense of worthiness that is full of self-importance, of arrogance or pride in self. Yet at the same time I remember the word of Shunryu Suzuki: "We are all perfect as we are." So these two sayings reflect two sides of the one reality of our life, of ourselves. We need to see and accept the preciousness of our life but also see and accept our shortcomings.

### Father Columba Stewart

In his chapter on humility, Benedict sketches a series of rather daunting steps to achieve that quality which for him is his preferred way of speaking of human integration and transformation. There are a couple of those steps that I think are crucial for this quality I call "compunction." One is the seventh degree of humility: to regard the self as worse than others, to be of no account, to be a worm and not a human being. To this is joined the twelfth step, where one stands as if already at the fearful judgment of God, saying over and over in the heart, "I am a sinner, not worthy to look up to you." This is a stance of profound awareness of all the alienation and unworthiness that one has ever felt, and also a profound awareness of where some of that might have come from. To borrow from the wonderful phrase of the Eastern Orthodox Starets Silouane, "We must cultivate the ability to hold our heart in hell and not despair."

The trick with compunction, if it is to be healthy, is that it is not simply a matter of dwelling on the sense of alienation and unworthiness. No, the trick of compunction is always to place that profound awareness of suffering within the much broader context of God's love. This requires a deep equipoise that allows us to stand in that place, profoundly aware of all that we have done, all the suffering that we have experienced, all the suffering that we have inflicted on others. But the beauty of it is that we need not be afraid to stand there.

So, speaking from a Christian perspective, I want to suggest that the feelings of unworthiness and alienation are feelings that we can never fully surrender, at least for most of us, in our experience of this life. But we can, in the equipoise of com-punction, put them in tension with that profound sense of where we have come from and where we are going. If we are able to accept ourselves in this way, and accept God's love for us as we are, the fruit of that experience is compassion for our-selves and for others. Truly healthy compunction is the aware-ness that the suffering I have inflicted on others, that I have experienced myself, can be for me a door into something vaster. Of course, the key to that door is love.

### Father Mark Delery

As I look back at my career as a monk, much of my time has been spent as a counselor. I've seen many people in many phases of suffering. About ten years ago, a woman approached me and said, "Do you remember the advice you gave me when I was a college senior?" I didn't remember, and I was sweating because I thought maybe I had told her not to get married. But then she told me that my advice to her was "Agree to be vul-nerable." She had guided her life by that simple advice for twenty years and was now applying and being accepted by a Trappistine monastery.

When I give this advice about agreeing to be vulnerable, it is to help people with self-acceptance. To accept ourselves, we have to accept the truth about ourselves, and that means being vulnerable. When people are going through divorces, or suffering from cancer or some other painful situation, they are being asked to turn themselves over in true vulnerability to God the Father in imitation of his divine Son. When they stop being aggressive toward what is troubling them in order to protect themselves from vulnerability, they can gradually accept their vulnerability and find a gentle place where they can discover more freedom and dignity.

### Judith Simmer-Brown

One of the Tibetan teachings that probably puts the most surprising sort of twist on understanding the feeling of unworthiness comes from Shantideva. He says that not feeling worthy carries a kind of discouragement, which can then be used as an excuse for laziness. One thing is to look at the causes of low self-esteem; another thing is to see how we might use it as an excuse for not doing things. For example, one might think, "I don't feel like I am worthy of that good job, so I will not take it." Spotting this kind of laziness in myself was a real shock to me!

### Joseph Goldstein

There are some classical Buddhist teachings about hindrances, one of which is called sloth and torpor. This hindrance is not simply sleepiness, dullness, or tiredness. It is a deep tendency to retreat from difficulties rather than advancing into them. We can use our sense of unworthiness as an excuse to retreat from life, from advancing in human maturity and spiritual progress. At one point in my practice, I reminded myself to "Choose the difficult." This mantra helped me to work with this particular hindrance of sloth or laziness.

### Geshe Lobsang Tenzin

The sense of unworthiness is also related to alienation, which is an underlying factor to many of the problems in our society at this time. From the Buddhist point of view, I think that one of the things that helps overcome both a sense of unworthiness and alienation is recognizing a common bond with others. As His Holiness the Dalai Lama would say, it's about recognizing that we all belong to the same humanity, all wishing to be happy and to avoid suffering.

Alienation also affects us on a spiritual level. We can feel alienated from ultimate reality. We can feel that we just do not fit in this world, or that God is against us in some way. So, I think it's essential to recognize that one aspect of our bond with others is that we all share the same nature. In Buddhism this would be called recognizing the Buddha-nature within. Or our Christian brothers and sisters might call it God within. In both cases it is important to know that we are not alone. It is important to recognize a deeper unity with humanity and with the divine ground of life itself. This unity strengthens our sense of worthiness and our hope for belonging. It means that we and everyone else have the potential to find peace and joy.

### Abbot John Daido Loori

It is common for students who are entering our monastic community to at first feel on the outside. They tend to isolate themselves, and then they complain that they are isolated. The thing that I try to get them to appreciate, that helps transform this situation, is that the alienation is really a mental process. It's not something that someone is doing to them but something that they create in the way they use their minds. The creation of the self, the unworthy self or in this case the alienated self, is a mental process.

Of course, all of the parts of that process are things that we do in dealing with our situation. When we take responsibility for that, when we own it, when we say, "I am creating this," we then enter a whole other realm, which is empowerment. We are no longer victims. We become empowered to do something more constructive about our situation and our lives. It's the same with other painful states of mind. Take anger, for example. If you just say, "He made me angry," there is nothing you can do about the anger. But when you realize that only you can make yourself angry, then you've empowered yourself to do something about your anger. And to me, that is real transformation.

### Venerable Henepola Gunaratana

We all feel one time or another that we are not accepted. We have feelings of worthlessness, alienation, sadness, and maybe anger and hatred. But underneath all these feelings is a subtle hope that we can be free from that feeling of not being acceptable. To realize this hope, we often do things to become acceptable in the eyes of others. This can lead to trouble, as we all know.

At the same time, we become attached to the unacceptable self-image we have and then blame others for it. If we learn to let go of our clinging to this sense of unacceptability, we can strengthen our self-acceptance, regardless of what others may think of us. We need to take responsibility for our problem and realize that the solving of our problem is within us. We cannot just blame anybody in the world for our inability to accept ourselves. Someone else may have made us feel this way in the first place, but we are the ones who are clinging to that self-concept. I strongly believe that when we learn to overcome our attachment to our ego-concept, then a sense of unworthiness will not become a problem. We will be happy to be who we are even if others have different opinions about us. It is our acceptance of ourselves that is the key to freedom. Then we can truly live loving friendliness, compassion, joy, and equanimity.

꒰

### Zenkei Blanche Hartman

Our work is letting go of holding on to our false self, our wrong view of the existence of a separate self. No one can let go of it for us. But as we see how much suffering it causes us, it gets easier to let it go. Dogen Zenji says, "Those who are enlightened about delusion, we call Buddhas. Those who are deluded about enlightenment, we call ordinary beings." If we realize that the delusion of a separate false self continually arises, as we see it arising, we can say, "Uh-oh," and let it go. It does continually arise, and we get in trouble when we grasp it and think it's real. When we recognize our connection with everything, it helps us to let go of that sense of separate selfhood. We feel supported by everything in our letting go.

Master Dogen said, "No gaining idea. We sit for the sake of sitting." If we are Buddha from the beginningless beginning, why do we sit? It is not to get something that we don't already have. We are already complete. There is nothing to get from outside. What our effort is about is to find in ourselves that basic goodness that is our birthright. We do not get it from someone else.

### Ajahn Amaro

One of the great Buddhist masters in Thailand, who has also been engaged in Christian-Buddhist dialogue over the years, is Venerable Buddhadasa. Once he said that the cross is a perfect spiritual symbol since it's like the letter "I" crossed out. Seeing the truth about ourselves, accepting ourselves, and letting go of ourselves are so central to our spiritual path. It is in this accepting and letting go of self that we discover loving kindness and compassion, and the doorway to freedom.

### Zoketsu Norman Fischer

People want to take up a spiritual practice because there is pain in their hearts. We need to recognize that pain is beneficial because it leads a person to make a change in his or her life. But the change that is needed is not to gain something but to let go. Spiritual practice does improve one's life, but you cannot pursue it for that reason—in order to gain something that you think you don't already have.

### Joseph Goldstein

One of the things that happens in extended Buddhist meditation practice is a tremendous refinement of our perception of change. When we begin to see this whole mind/body/heart process as arising and vanishing instantaneously, there is no solidity, nothing to hold on to, nothing to grasp at. It's in the seeing of this directly, not conceptually but as we are actually experiencing that microscopic momentariness, that we discover there is no place for comparison to others to be rooted. It's through the doorway of impermanence that we really get a very deep taste of what selflessness means. Nothing lasts long enough to be a solid self. It's in that sense that acceptance allows for a new balance of mind.

One of the interesting discoveries that we make in meditation practice, and we know this also at the therapeutic psychological level, is that resistance feeds the very thing that we are resisting. If we have judgment about ourselves, the judgments themselves are locking us in to what we don't like about ourselves. So the path of purification goes through the doorway of self-acceptance. Through acceptance, the mind relaxes; and through that relaxation of mind, we see this incredibly fast flow of change. As we see the change, the mind doesn't grasp. And in the nongrasping, the letting go, there is freedom.

### Stephanie Kaza

Greed for ideals has perhaps been the biggest plague in my life. Making your spiritual life into a religious career path toward gaining more and more of what you are seeking is a particular pitfall for people with religious ideals. There is a great liberation in realizing that we are like Coyote, always foolish and always fallible. Here, too, letting go is the antidote. The key is to hold our ideals without spiritual greed.

### Father Leo Lefebure

A number of years ago, a young priest in Central America, Oscar Romero, had a tremendous struggle with perfectionism. He had a very rigid standard of how he was supposed to be, and along with it a tremendous sense of his own unworthiness, a sense of shame. He threw himself into his work, but it did not help; and his relationships with other people suffered. He ended up being diagnosed by a psychiatrist as having an obsessive-compulsive disorder. He then tried even harder to get it right and threw himself into his work all the more, but it all seemed to be going nowhere.

Despite these emotional problems, Romero was chosen to be archbishop of El Salvador. Perhaps he was an attractive candidate because he was so concerned about what others thought about him. A few weeks after he was named archbishop, a Jesuit priest, Rutilio Grande, was killed together with a couple of his companions because of their work for the poor. That night Oscar Romero went to the church where the bodies of these three persons were lying; and when he looked at them, he saw something he had never seen before. He looked at those bodies and saw the presence of Christ. This experience so changed him that he turned to the people who were gathered there, many of them friends of the people who were slain, and asked, "Where do we go from here?"

From that point on his whole life changed. He was able to see Christ in the suffering poor of El Salvador. He took up the image of the suffering servant from the second part of the Book of Isaiah, which originally was a personification of the people of Israel during the Babylonian Captivity. These people were despised, humiliated, shamed by all the other more powerful nations. But they were the ones on whom God's favor rested, and it was through them that blessings come to the nations.

Christians understand this in terms of the life of Jesus. Oscar Romero took this image and applied it to the suffering poor in El Salvador, and from then on the struggle with perfectionism was gone. All the worry about getting it right, all the worry about pleasing people, the worry about acceptance and his own unworthiness—all that was gone. He began speaking the truth as he saw it and did not care about the consequences. He was warned many times before he was finally murdered at the altar and became one of the great witnesses of the church in our times.

# CHAPTER EIGHT

# Freedom from Attachments

## FROM CONSUMERISM TO COMPASSION

### Geshe Lhundub Sopa

We all want happiness. But there are two levels of happiness. One is the physical happiness that comes from the enjoyment of our senses. We all enjoy beautiful sounds, sights, and smells. We all enjoy tasting good food and drink. We all enjoy touching things that bring pleasurable sensations. When we pursue physical happiness, we find that the pleasures of the senses are only temporary. They are tied to the amount of money and power we have. Therefore, we seek more power and money to enjoy more sensual pleasures. Soon that becomes our only goal in life. It gives our life purpose.

For religious people, we too enjoy the pleasures of the senses—we are all human beings. But we don't let these enjoyments define our identity as persons. We seek another kind of happiness, a spiritual happiness that is not temporary. It is an inner peace that is there whether we are enjoying pleasure or not. Every religion has this kind of spiritual peace and happiness as a goal. Religious teachings and teachers are guides in the search for spiritual liberation, spiritual happiness.

Yet we are humans who live in the world of sensations. So we need to consume certain products to meet our needs. In this sense, consumer products are necessary. The real question here is motivation. In our consumption, are we motivated by selfishness? Are we seeking happiness only in our consumption?

Shantideva said that spiritual prayer and a life of compassion are like powerful medicines. Like a good cure, they serve two purposes. On one hand, they are antidotes to the sickness of seeking happiness through sensual attachment to things. On the other hand, they bring us true happiness, true peace of mind. They lead us in our minds and hearts to find the real source of happiness that we already have but do not know it.

*Sister Kathy Lyzotte*

One of the insidious dangers resulting from consumerism is the undermining of a person's identity. A consumer-oriented culture, with continuous advertising, tends to address the individual as no more than a potential customer and so reduces the human person to being simply a consumer. And this is what our marketing society is all about: getting customers and making sales. The message is "You are what you buy." People identify with certain brand names and form an attachment to them and then get their identity from the image with which the brand is associated.

Meanwhile, forces of isolation are strong. A highly mobile society leads to a loss of geographical roots and a sense of rootlessness. Having lost our identity as part of a local community, our sense of belonging and connectedness to people is greatly weakened. Figures portrayed in the media often seem much more interesting than real people, and virtual reality seems more exciting than daily life. Facts and information seem to eclipse the loving knowledge derived from authentic human interactions. And so the temptation is to purchase commodities in order to achieve a sense of belonging.

Counteracting these dehumanizing forces, Christianity offers the human being a faith-based identity through baptism. This sacrament of Christian initiation signifies and brings about a person's living relationship with the triune God, which is actualized throughout the course of a human lifetime. Baptism also initiates a person into the Christian faith community, giving the person a new identity as a member of the church. We often take this for granted; but this is the necessary foundation of a dedicated life. As we grow in love and communion with one another, we also find the peace and satisfaction that consumerism promises and does not deliver.

Christianity has always affirmed the dignity of the human person. My identity as a baptized Christian is that of someone who is loved by God. Christian faith is most basically a faith in the love that God has for me, for each human being, for all of humanity. My faith in this gratuitous and redemptive love enables me to love God and to love other people. Love, then, is the deepest meaning of it all. This is exactly what my community prays in the opening prayer on the morning of Good Friday: "Love is the deepest meaning of it all"—love as personal relationships, as communion, as mutual indwelling.

Christian faith, then, leads us to the realm of mystery and to a very fundamental truth: the truth that the separate self is an illusion and the truth that loving communion of persons is the ultimate reality. These two statements are really one truth; they affirm the need for single isolated individuals to transcend themselves, overcome greed and selfishness in love and communion. There would be no more place for greed and a consumeristic mind-set if people really felt fulfilled, felt that they have everything because of their participation in the depths of this mystery.

❧

### Father James Wiseman

Some time ago the *Washington Post* had a front-page article that began with an account of a young man in New York who had amassed a fortune of $60 million during the heady days of the stock-market boom. During that time the man started a Web TV venture in his residence, a huge loft on lower Broadway. The entire place, including bedrooms and bathrooms, was outfitted with Web cameras to record his every move. He threw nightlong parties, set up a machine-gun shooting range in the basement, and traveled to nearby sites in rented helicopters. When the bubble in technology stocks burst, he saw his fortune quickly diminish by nearly 98 percent and decided to leave New York for an ashram in India. Why? "I really need to reconnect," he said. "This dream's over."

It would be easy for us simply to say that this man got his comeuppance for such ostentatious living, but it would be more salutary to ask if there isn't something we can all learn from this story. Is there not an ongoing need to "reconnect" even on the part of those of us who have allegedly spurned the pursuit of wealth by taking monastic vows? Isn't this what is demanded of Benedictines and Cistercians by the vow of *conversatio morum,* that not easily translatable promise to seek ever-deeper fidelity to the monastic way of life, the never-ending call to continuing conversion?

No doubt few of us have ever had anything even approaching the amount of wealth that that New Yorker once had, but one of the most enduring lessons that we can learn from the fathers and mothers of the fourth-century Egyptian desert is that the telltale indicator of greed isn't the size or value of the object coveted but rather the tenacity with which one clings to it. That great religious psychologist John Cassian, who himself spent some years among these desert monastics and later wrote about their lives and teachings in his *Institutes* and *Conferences,* often points out how ridiculous it is to have given up all the big things mentioned in the Gospel—home, land, spouse—and then become agitated if there appears the danger of losing something as minor as a pen or knife.

How true this is! And how often might we not have to admit that we have fallen prey to this kind of passion. We usually regard it as normal for children to plead anxiously for their parents to buy them this or that toy and then jealously watch out lest their playmates take the toy from them. I still remember very well how, as a young boy, I once kept pestering my mother until she bought me a particular board game. Needless to say, my fascination with the game didn't last all that long; the next month I wanted something else, and the game was relegated to the dust of the attic.

We may smile at such behavior in children, but how sad it is when the same sort of greedy attitude is found in supposedly mature adults. It is, as Cassian said, a "passion," and his Latin word could just as well be translated as "a suffering." It is something that we undergo and that afflicts us by drawing us away from our true center and goal, what the Gospel calls the Kingdom or "the one thing necessary" (Luke 10:42), which is ultimately the God of whom St. Augustine famously said: "You have created us for yourself, and our hearts are restless until they rest in you."

### Venerable Guo Yuan Fa Shi

Our teacher distinguishes between our wants and our needs. Our wants are always in the forefront of our minds. We are always processing our desires as we live our daily lives. Becoming aware of our needs takes some extra work. We have to sort through all our wants to see what it is that we actually need. When we do this, we find that we need very little. So, our teacher has made the suggestion that if you entertain a want, don't just go out and get it. Ask yourself first, "Do I really need this?" Only if you can answer "Yes" should you buy it.

Why should we be so careful in this regard? Because we are dealing with one of the most powerful and subtle of the Three Poisons, namely greed. Greed is very deep-rooted and often out of our sight. But even if we do not see it, it is affecting our lives and the lives of others. It promises happiness but cannot give us what it promises. That is the problem. Because if happiness does not come from getting something we want, greed tells us that we need to possess even more to find happiness. And this process goes on and on, with no true happiness ever really emerging.

One other way of dealing with our possessions is to see them as blessings. When we have something, we should not say, "This is mine. I earned this through my hard work." In some sense that may be true. But there are many factors that are out of our control that contribute to obtaining our possessions. So we should say with humility and gratefulness, "This is a blessing." If we have a sense that what we have are blessings, then we will be more sensitive to those who do not have what they need. They too do not control their destiny, so they can use our help in meeting their needs. Then we can be more generous in helping them.

### Stephanie Kaza

Last year I invented a new course called "Unlearning Consumerism." The students were extremely responsive to our work with consumerism as an addiction. We had support groups around weekly CD binges, coffee addictions, and clothing obsessions. One of the things we observed is that it is very hard to find a place where these products are not being advertised constantly. Today students are dealing with consumerism on MTV as well as on the Internet. Maybe one role for monasteries is to become consumerism detox zones, away from the constant stimulation of advertising that reinforces our addiction.

### Sister Kathy Lyzotte

A healthy community life, as well as a healthy family life, can be a buffer between the individual and consumer-oriented society at large. Parish communities, religious orders, membership in nonprofit organizations—all of these forms of small community go far to foster real life-giving bonds among individuals and promote a sense of trust and security that reduces dependency on commodities. In monastic community life, our needs are taken care of, real needs and not just wants, and so we learn to discern and to moderate our desires.

Healthy community and family life teaches temperance, helps to reduce possessiveness, leads to sharing and caring for more than oneself, and unites people in a common cause with an emphasis that goes beyond the material. Being called by name and called to account, we learn to be responsible and to take responsibility. Communal celebrations express the gratefulness and joy of life together in receptive openness to divine mystery. This is the value of community and family life at its best.

Our tradition teaches us not to scapegoat, not to judge, and not to condemn either ourselves or others, but in humbleness of heart to hear the call to repentance and continual conversion. Like Job, the rich man in the Bible who was tested by God yet maintained his innocence, we have to open up to the sufferings that come to us. We need to resist the temptation to escape into consumer products and to see our difficulties as divine interventions, letting go of arguments and rationalizations, responding first with an inner silence that is the source of wisdom.

What is wisdom for Christians? In a way that seems to resonate with Buddhism, James says, "The wisdom from above is first of all pure, peaceable, gentle, compliant, full of mercy and good fruits, without inconstancy or insincerity" (James 3:17). At one point in *Conjectures of a Guilty Bystander,* Thomas Merton

quotes these words of Gandhi: "A person who realizes the particular evil of his time and finds that it overwhelms him, dives
deep in his own heart for inspiration, and when he gets it he
presents it to others."

### Ajahn Sundara

There are several teachings in the Theravada tradition that address the issue of money and how to use it skillfully. If one's
livelihood is not motivated by greed or ill will, and does not
bring harm, then gaining wealth is acceptable. But the question
is: How is one motivated in the use of the wealth? The correct motivation is to use the wealth to benefit others, to develop the virtues of generosity, selflessness, and compassion. In
Buddhism, generosity is considered one of the most important
qualities of the heart. It is listed as the first of the Ten Spiritual
Perfections. Our advice to people of wealth, following the
teaching of the Buddha, is to use it to benefit others, and you
too will be benefited. Generosity is the door of the heart
through which one can free oneself from selfishness.

### Abbot John Daido Loori

One of the steps in the Eightfold Path is "Right Livelihood." The Buddha says that Right Livelihood means pursuing a living that will not harm others. In pursuing this living, one should not be motivated to make more than one needs. If work is done to gain money to buy luxuries, one's craving and attachments increase, and one can more easily become willing to deceive or to exploit others to get ahead. On the other hand, by working to make a living and to serve others, one can also advance in the spiritual life by becoming freer of attachments and growing in compassion and loving kindness.

We try to carry out our businesses at our monastery according to these teachings of the Buddha, and right now they are making a profit. Work is part of our practice. We try in our work to be sensitive to the real needs of those we are serving, rather than trying to generate new desires for our products. If someone does not have the means to buy one of our products, we give it to him or her. Now we are holding workshops to help others outside the monastery apply the principles of Right Livelihood. And we are finding that many people in business are interested in what we are doing. It is a way to make a living and not become consumed by the very process of making a living.

### Zoketsu Norman Fischer

All people, religious and nonreligious, know that advertising whips up people's greed, which is true. The thing is, we are all supported by the consumer system in which advertising plays a key role. Through this system in a globalized world market, the wealth of some—created on the backs of many—is generated by the ever-increasing need for stuff. The problem is that the world economy would collapse if there weren't this ever-increasing need for more stuff, which is generated by the advertising that gets people interested in buying more things.

Spiritually, we can all see the dangers of this system. But think of what would happen if we simplified our lives, it we cut back on consuming. The economy would grind to a halt, and people around the world lose their jobs. So I think we are facing a very difficult global problem. It is as if we have painted ourselves into a corner. To mix metaphors, it seems that we have sown the seeds of greed, and now we are caught in the web of consumerism.

### Judith Simmer-Brown

There is an International Buddhist-Christian Theological Encounter that has met annually since 1984. It was founded by John Cobb and Masao Abe. For the past several years, we have been discussing social issues like consumerism and globalization. These are such powerful forces in the world today.

Most of our institutions have bought into them or have been bought by them. So now there are very few places where there is real concern about the damage being done to our communities and our world through the powers of consumerism and globalization.

Consumerism and globalization are not just individual forces, they are interconnected systems that magnify our human wants. Using our notion of dependent origination, there is a kind of global consumer web in which many people feel they are caught. They feel helpless and hopeless in facing it. But we know that in dependent origination, there are definite causes and conditions for why things are what they are. We need to look carefully at the web and try to discern the causes and conditions that have set it up in order to discover ways of liberation.

There is much pain now in the world due to these economic forces. In the developing nations we can see this clearly in the sweatshops, the deforestation, the destruction of local economies, and so on. But also here in the United States, consumerism on the other end is moving us to define ourselves only as workers and consumers. As for causes, corporations and institutions are given special rights and privileges globally, free from government regulations.

Where is the space for asking questions concerning what it all means and how solutions can be found? There are organizations doing this. But it seems that the monastery can provide us with a spiritual vantage point from which to look at what is happening, a vantage point that is not so sullied by the new environment of consumerism and globalization.

### Father Daniel Ward

When it's a question of the monastic response to consumerism, it's not so much a matter of how individual monastics respond but how the institution responds. In the United States, a number of religious communities are trying to look at the right use of property. They're asking how they should use their property in ways that preserve the environment and that don't cause people to suffer or overconsume. To me this is where the issue is. It's not so much with my individuality; it's with the community, with the religious institution. We all, monastics and laypersons, need to find ways of helping our institutions make more responsible decisions regarding the use of money and resources.

### Prioress Mary Collins

Consumerism and individualism is systemic, and religious institutions are very much a part of their culture. We all need to find ways of fostering a culture of communion, of unity and sharing. Most of us come from monasteries that are well established, have received gifts from wealthy friends, and count on that kind of support. I think that somehow or other the teachings and the practices that we've had—the restricted use of personal funds, the one bar of soap at a time—don't really address the question of how we can be more in communion with one another in a global way. They don't address how we can share what we have to feed the hungry, to address poverty, to create new forms of society that will be more just.

I respect the fact that spiritual motivation is very important and that the question of dealing with suffering in terms of attitude may be appropriate as a responsibility for me to take on for myself. But I cannot say to my brother or sister in India, "It's just a matter of mind over matter." The world in which they live is a world that is in great need, and there is no way to provide for this need using our present systems.

### Sister Kathy Lyzotte

Faced with the issues of greed and consumerism, it is too easy for religious people like myself to scapegoat and denounce Wall Street, large corporations, global marketing, or capitalism in general, seeing only the dehumanized surface, overlooking the faithful service to society of hardworking people in many occupations. The tendency to blame and denounce the business world may be one of the occupational hazards of those of us in organized religion.

When I first began to reflect on the evils of capitalism, I thought there would be plenty to denounce. But in the course of sitting with this topic, reading and grappling with the issues, I began to see other aspects. I concluded that I myself am a participant in consumer society, that our monasteries are part of the economic system. I understood that dialogue, repen-

tance, and conversion are effective responses to our consumer
culture, both for individuals and institutions.

❧

### Venerable Thubten Chodron

It is true that when we turn to spirituality, we think that we are
leaving behind the corruption of the world, the culture of
greed and consumerism, for a higher purpose. But our old way
of thinking does not just disappear; it follows us into our spiritual practice and colors it, as well. Since we have all been
raised to be good consumers, getting the most while paying
the least, as teachers and students of the spiritual life, we carry
our consumer mentality into our spiritual practice.

So, first of all, from the side of the student, we want the
best product so we want the best spirituality. We shop around
for the best teacher, the highest practice or teaching. But we
also want it with the least amount of effort. We like instant
gratification. So we seek the practice that will get us most
quickly and easily to the ultimate spiritual goal.

Another factor of consumerism is that we want to be en-
tertained. Spiritual teachers should definitely entertain us, and
if they do not we might go somewhere else. In my Tibetan tradition, many exotic things keep us from being bored. There are
high thrones for our teachers, brocade seat covers, tablecloths
and robes, long horns, short horns, bells, drums, and, oh yes,
hats . . . yellow ones, red ones, and black ones!

Another thing we consumers expect is comfort. Things should be easily available, so we don't have to put forth much effort to get the teachings we need. In ancient times, people traveled over the Himalayan Mountains, across the Silk Road, and went through all sorts of hardships to find teachers. But nowadays, we want our teachers to come to us. And we expect to hear their teachings in a nice comfortable room, at the right temperature, and with good food. We shouldn't have to undergo any difficulties.

We often go into the spiritual domain with the consumerist thought: "What can *I* get out of this? How is this going to benefit *me*?" We want to get something for ourselves. "Teachers should give me what I want because it's a matter of supply and demand."

We want to have spiritual status. We may get it by being close to a teacher. We also gain some status by getting all the Dharma paraphernalia. We all have gift shops, where you have all sorts of beautiful statues of Buddhas or bodhisattvas, and all kinds of offering objects. As good consumers, especially when we enter the practice, we get all this stuff so we can feel like we are really religious people.

But maybe, just maybe, religious practice is about giving, not getting. It is hard to entertain that thought if our thinking is molded by consumerism. An Asian Buddhist temple in Houston held a summer camp for children. People worked in the kitchen, cooking food for a hundred kids for five days. They were there to give, not get. It was part of the spiritual practice, and they were happy, they relished those days of pure service to children.

The consumer mentality also influences the mind of the teacher. Our advertising boasts about the excellent qualities of our teachers. Most ads display enticing photos of the teacher, who is proclaimed to be a fully accomplished master with the most exotic teaching. "You can't miss this teaching because it's only given to a select group of students and only costs $99.99!"

Also, from the side of the teacher, the success of one's course, teaching, or retreat is measured in numbers. In consumerism, we measure success in numbers: "So, how many students came to the retreat? Did I get more students than the other teacher, who was also teaching a retreat the same weekend? Who is more popular? Do I have more students? Are my retreats better attended? How much offering did I receive? Because, after all, we are building a center. We need funds."

As teachers, we feel the need to make our spiritual traditions appealing to consumers, because if it isn't appealing, then they are going to take their business somewhere else. And we can't have that. So we might water down the teachings or leave out certain points to make it more appealing so that more people come.

I have to ask "Isn't all the hype, the dressing up of the teachings, the selling of the teacher, totally going contrary to what Buddhism is all about? Are we really being true to the deep spiritual lineages in which we've been trained, or are we just making things available in a consumer way to a large number of people so everybody buys our product?"

I personally believe that this consumer approach to spirituality in the West makes our own spiritual traditions degenerate in a number of ways. First of all, we are not practicing what we are teaching. Eventually people are going to ask "What's going on? Do these teachings really work? I don't see it in what is going on here." Second, by watering down the teachings, future generations won't get the purity of what we have received. So it is harmful for the transmission of our faith to the future as well as to us as practitioners.

As religious practitioners, the basic foundation of what we are trying to do is go beyond a happiness found in consuming the things of this life. We are trying to reach a deeper truth that opens our hearts and extends love and compassion to everybody. It is in this realization of our deepest potential as human beings that we find lasting contentment, real happiness. This is the appropriate meaning of "success" in religious practice, not our wealth, number of students, or fame.

### Venerable Henepola Gunaratana

Sometimes Buddhist teachers start their teaching career with a pure heart, with the right motivation, with skillful intention, without having any intention of gaining popularity or gaining wealth. They begin purely out of the conviction that they want to share the Dharma, the Teaching, with others, without seeking any personal gains. Eventually, because of the teacher's pure heart, the message becomes very effective and people are drawn to the teacher. The teacher never expects those things, and yet people are drawn by his or her example. Then word gets around, and more and more people come. At that point, if the teacher becomes attached to his or her new reputation, these things will become an impediment. The mental states of pride and arrogance are always there to be stimulated by our personal gains. There is a kind of spiritual ambition that can drive our ego in the religious life. It is very dangerous and we need to be mindfully aware of it.

### Reverend Heng Sure

The Buddha's Dharma, or Teaching, in the West is so new that it is no surprise that the people look at it as a kind of spiritual product. Television has so many consumer messages each day telling us that we are not complete until we acquire their product. That is strong, strong conditioning. So, if a religion says that it has something that will improve your life, we think that what it offers must be like a product.

On the other hand, many of the young people who come to our monastery are largely postalcohol, postdrugs, postconsumer. They have tried all the products out there and cannot find what they are looking for. They have left the marketplace and are quite cynical. We call them "postdespair," their weariness is so great. They are not looking for a new product, and they may be largely inarticulate in describing what they actually are looking for. My thought is that they are looking for something true. The Dharma cuts through the static of the marketing messages and rings true.

### Father James Wiseman

That longtime best-seller by M. Scott Peck, *The Road Less Traveled,* has a marvelous passage in which he recounts a discussion in a couples' group in which it became obvious to him that the participants looked at the purpose and function of their spouses simply in reference to themselves. All of them failed to perceive that their mates might have an existence basically separate from their own or any kind of destiny apart from their marriage. We can see here the result of our individualism, our desire to find fulfillment in the possession of other things or persons.

If this isn't recognized, whether in a marriage or in a friendship, then it becomes all too easy for the other person to be valued only for what he or she can give to oneself. This kind of possessiveness is far worse than that which pertains to inanimate objects. For here what is coveted or grasped has feelings of his or her own, so now two persons suffer, though in different ways. Treating others and valuing them as possessions does real violence to their personhood, who they really are as people.

One of my favorite spiritual writers, the late Eknath Easwaran, put this very well in his book *Words to Live By* when he said:

> *Jealousy comes into a relationship when we try to possess someone for ourselves. It is a very difficult secret to discover: that when we do not want to possess another person selfishly, when we do not make demand after demand, the relationship will grow and last. And it is something we have to learn the hard, hard way. This is the secret of all relationships, not only between husband and wife, boyfriend and girlfriend, but between friend and friend, parents and children.*

As I look back on relationships in my own life, the ones that have endured and flourished were precisely the ones that lacked a dimension of possessiveness. The ones that went sour were usually marked by the kind of selfish "demand after demand" of which Eknath Easwaran wrote, whether I was on the giving or the receiving end of the demands. One of the greatest gifts we can give to someone we cherish is to refrain from imprisoning them within the web of our own expectations, desires, or needs. Just think how much less suffering there would be in the world if we all really understood this and lived accordingly!

# CHAPTER NINE

# Overcoming Violence

## FROM ANGER TO COMMUNION

### Geshe Lobsang Tenzin

Violence is a plague that affects our society today. Of course, we have experienced violence throughout history, but at this time we are experiencing new forms of inhuman violence: violence created by schoolchildren, horrible acts of terrorism, ethnic cleansing, violence against women and girls in the sex trade, and so on.

When we look at the problem in its totality, it seems that a solution is out of our reach. But I think that it is precisely at the time when these problems seem so large that peo-

ple begin to look beyond just political and legal solutions
to their own spiritual traditions for answers. I come from a
Buddhist tradition, and would like to share some insights that
the Buddha and his followers have proposed concerning violence.

His Holiness the Dalai Lama, in a brief statement, says that
"violence means any action that is motivated by hatred."
Hatred is an emotional response that arises due to our inability
to accept difficulties or to forgive those who cause difficulties.
Faced with these unwanted conditions, we become angry, hatred is directed toward the persons or things that cause these
difficult conditions, and violence is that hatred in action.

In the Abhidharma tradition of Buddhist thought, it is said
that for any unwholesome action—violence, for example—
there must be five factors: the basis, the motivation, the emotion behind that motivation, the actual execution or action, and
the actual completion of the action. The primary basis of violence is hatred; but other emotions, such as greed or jealousy,
can also contribute to the motivation. In the case of violence,
that motivation is the willful intention to harm a person.

How does Buddhism say that we can short-circuit this
mental process so that the actual execution of a violent action
does not happen? How can we produce a process that leads to
nonviolence, and how can this inner process of thought and
feeling be integrated in one's personal life? In addressing these
questions, His Holiness the Dalai Lama usually suggests what
is known in the Tibetan tradition as *view and action*. That is,
while our violent actions are expressions of hatred, we need to
look at where the hatred is coming from. We need to look at

our views or perceptions about the difficult situations that move us to anger, hatred, and violence.

When we look at our mental orientation in addressing difficult situations, we discover that we experience mental unrest. This mental unrest arises from a perceived obstruction to what we want. That is to say, anybody or anything that is perceived as creating an obstacle for our own pleasure, reputation, wealth, and so on—that person or thing generates within us a certain kind of mental unrest. Shantideva calls this mental unrest a discomfort that arises from perceived obstacles to what we desire.

Now, these perceived obstacles need not be just to the realization of my own desires, but also to those of my family, my friends, my country, my religion. You know, it is very hard to draw a line between me and those things or persons with which or whom I identify myself. Some of the terrible violence that we are facing now is violence in the name of families, races, nations, and religions. They all seem to arise due to people perceiving that somebody else is obstructing or causing harm to that with which they identify themselves. So, violence as an expression of hatred has to be fundamentally dealt with by cultivating a mental ease in the presence of perceived obstacles to our desired goals. For that reason, valid perception, proper understanding, is of crucial importance.

His Holiness the Dalai Lama says that the proper Buddhist understanding of dependent origination supports the conduct of nonviolence. Nonviolence is a logical outcome of the proper understanding of dependent arising as the nature of reality. So, let me say a little bit about how the understanding of dependent arising can help in overcoming personal or communal violence.

Dependent arising, from a Buddhist point of view, has to be understood on various levels. One level has to do with causal dependence. That is to say, everything that comes to be arises dependent upon a number of causes and conditions. That being the case, the problems, difficulties, and obstacles we face have more than one cause. It is natural for us to judge a particular person or group as the sole cause of our problems. But, in fact, there are many causes and conditions to take into consideration and to address. Some of these causal aspects may include things that we have done ourselves. A good example of how this is so can be seen in the conflict between Palestine and Israel.

On another level, we need to look at ourselves, our own attitudes and behavior. What we will find is that we are conditioned by many unwholesome attitudes and are engaged in many unhealthy actions. We too participate in ways of thinking, speaking, and acting that contribute to humanity's all-pervasive condition of suffering. From this point of view, we can understand more clearly that we too have to assume a certain responsibility for the problems of humankind.

If we can look at our unhappy condition from both of these levels of dependent arising, we can realize that the person or persons we blame for our troubles are not the only ones responsible and that we too share in the responsibility for our world's troubling condition. This insight can give rise to a sense of compassion, even for those who present us with obstacles to what we want out of life. And this compassion is a

real antidote for persons and for communities. If we can cultivate and promote compassion through a deeper sense of connectedness, hope for reducing violence seems more realistic.

꙰

## Donald Mitchell

In the late 1980s, I was asked to meet with His Holiness the
Dalai Lama to convey some information to him. I did so, and
in the process he listened very attentively and politely. But I
was not quite sure how interested he was until I began to inform him about some activities for youth. These activities were
helpful for lay spiritual formation, for helping to strengthen a
child's character and sense of self-worth. At this point in the
conversation, His Holiness became quite animated.

He asked whether we were teaching doctrines or values.
When I answered that the emphasis was on living one's faith
in daily life with focus on love and unity, he said, "This is very,
very important because in the future, children are going to do
violent and terrible things." I listened to him give some examples of the kinds of violent acts that children would commit,
including murder. To tell the truth, at that time I could not believe what he was saying. Then years later came Columbine.

His Holiness also said that we can no longer just assume
that basic human values will be passed down from generation
to generation. As religious persons and institutions, we need to
find ways of helping laypeople guide their children in basic

moral living. It is fine to teach doctrine, but we must focus on how to live our faith, how to live what we believe in daily life. This means that spirituality cannot be reserved just for the monastery but must be shared with everyone and lived everywhere. This was also the message of His Holiness's friend Thomas Merton.

### Robert Aitken Roshi

I like the word "decent." It means "fitting and appropriate." Children learn to be decent to one another by the influence of parents and teachers. Societies learn to be decent by the influence of parents and teachers like the Buddha and the Christ.

The Thai Buddhist master Buddhadasa pointed out that the sun, moon, and stars live together as a cooperative and that our very bodily parts function as a cooperative. This is the ultimately fitting and appropriate way of the universe. He went on to warn that if our lives are not based on this kind of universal decency, then we shall all perish.

We tend to suffer and cause others to suffer in the most indecent fashion. We tend to conspire to build structures that camouflage our suffering, and others suffer the more. The Buddha observed, *"Dukkha, dukkha,* all is *dukkha." Dukkha* is usually translated "suffering," but David Loy, in his studies of politics and economics from a Buddhist perspective, suggests the word "lack."

With lack there is fear. I don't amount to anything at all, and my end is near. My family will not endure. My work, my ideas—all are evaporating like dewdrops on a lotus leaf. I fear this is your case as well, and the case of all beings. It's scary.

Liberation from *dukkha,* liberation from the fear of lack, the Buddha said, is a way of releasing oneself into the universe of selves. With just one step, you and I can realize that it's all right that we can't be stand-alone individuals, stand-alone families, stand-alone ethnic, economic, or national entities. We have set up profound anguish for ourselves and others by holding the contrary notion that such exclusive identity is possible. Liberation from this profoundly mistaken view is a path straight ahead, together with everyone and everything, in the great, dynamic ramble of life where differences are not boundaries.

This is no time for false modesty. Structural violence is today fueled by destructive technology and directed by criminals. The danger to people, animals, and plants escalates exponentially by the week. Our petty self-aggrandizement makes us miserable; national self-interest and corporate greed makes the world miserable.

It is surely high time that we enter into a process of purification. Let's you and me conspire with friends to vow each morning to practice the way of decency in our homes, our neighborhoods, and our workplaces and to follow through as best we can. Let's join our sisters and brothers who are already in the streets, and bang our pots for the human way that is fitting and appropriate to Earth and its beings. Let's organize for decency!

### Venerable Chuen Phangcham

It seems that the whole world is disturbed by violence. All beings, human and nonhuman, are experiencing violence and death in ways, and to degrees, that we have not seen in the past. From a Buddhist standpoint, the main causes of this violence are in the mind: anger, hatred, selfish desire, delusion, and ignorance. The great unrest we are experiencing in our minds is connected to a kind of carelessness. People are careless in the ways they think about, speak to, and behave with others. We see this all the time in the media. This carelessness also turns inward, and one becomes careless about oneself. People allow all sorts of evil to enter their minds, without caring what it does to them. Again we see this happening as people take in so many unhealthy things from the media.

A solution to this kind of carelessness is to become more mindful. Mindfulness can disperse our ignorance of how the world is affecting us and how we are affecting the world. We can become more mindful of how careless we are by taking in unhealthy ideas and attitudes, or of how careless we are by letting our feelings be affected by negative stimuli. We can also see more clearly how we are carelessly passing on unhealthy ideas and attitudes to others, even to our own children.

If we are more mindful, we will become more careful of our feelings of anger, fear, or hatred as they come into our mind. Being more caring, we will care more about what will happen if we allow those feelings to motivate our actions. So awareness and mindfulness are the keys to a more caring way of living that can enable people not to get caught in the web of violence.

### Samu Sunim

I do believe as a Buddhist that the root cause of violence is hatred. It is true that the lack of tolerance, the lack of patience, the lack of understanding, or sheer ignorance can easily contribute to violence. But I still think that the underlying cause is hatred: "I don't like that guy." So we need to look at the many Buddhist teachings directed toward removing ill will, animosity, malice, and hatred within us and within our world. These teachings dwell on compassion, loving kindness, generosity, and friendship as antidotes to the negative side of human nature.

The other day some people invited me to go to visit Lincoln's birthplace. A poster there displays different photographs taken of Lincoln throughout his lifetime. Above the photographs it says, "With malice towards none; with charity for all." To a Buddhist, this is very impressive! It reminds me of the bodhisattva in our own tradition who lives his or her whole life in this same way.

### Paul Gailey

When we create a situation that produces suffering for ourselves or others, there are different ways to respond to it. One response, if we fail to see our own role in creating the situation, is to blame someone else for the problems that result. Assigning blame in this way is in itself a form of violence and often propagates violent reactions. Another way to respond to the suffering we have created is to take responsibility, but without some form of self-flagellation, which can be an example of the "inner violence" Thomas Merton described. I find these distinctions to be critically important.

One of the great gifts offered by the contemplative traditions is the teaching that we must honestly recognize and address how the roots of the problems we see in the world penetrate our own lives as well. But we must find a way to reach this point without doing inner violence to ourselves.

### Prioress Mary Collins

Several years ago, a woman friend of mine who was an art teacher in a boys' prep school observed in midterm that the young men she taught in junior high and high school were resistant to working with art materials other than pencil, pen, and ink. She began musing on what was going on among them, for this behavior was unknown in her previous teaching experience. The boys disliked handling clay, wood, and woodworking tools, papier-mâché, and other art media that made messes. They did not like dirty hands. Slowly her judgment formed. Their resistance was a resistance to learning and dealing with the unknown properties of things. Why?

She thought of reasons. Perhaps it was because the boys were in the first generation in which childhood play had been primarily with electronic toys and not with sandboxes and cardboard boxes and mud. Perhaps it was because the intelligence that mattered in their schooling was rational, discursive, and linear intelligence, where insight was best communicated through ink on paper. In any case, because she was a good art teacher, she found ways to engage her students in handling clay and wood blocks. She thought their learning how real things like mud and sand work—what they can and cannot do—might have some long-term bearing on their future reverence for reality. Her musings left me thinking about the developmental consequences of welcoming or resisting "the properties of things."

Our culture does not welcome the notions that limits are inherent in every created thing. We have transformed the eighteenth-century political notion of inalienable rights into an unfettered right to whatever goods will give us pleasure and self-satisfaction. Like the adolescent sons of our culture, we are not interested in discovering the messy truths about the properties of things and learning to work with their reality. We are taught to be self-centered, self-assertive, self-protective. Whatever does not serve personal ego-ambition, contribute to our immediate pleasure, or enhance our comfort is liable to be devalued or subjected to the violence of our mishandling.

Rather than enduring the suffering inherent in facing limits, our unredeemed or unenlightened selves press on, violently imposing our wills on resisting realities, defying the odds. Everywhere around us we see humans refusing to accept the givenness of limited oil reserves, limited fresh water, limited longevity, limited fertility, or territorial limits. We see human communities refusing to accept the existence of other human communities with different values and aspirations distinct from theirs. Whether at the macroscale of global reality or the microscale of local human community, our resistance to the reality of limits causes us suffering, and that suffering evokes violence and abuse.

How can we break this cycle of human frustration, suffering, and violence? One of the inspired New Testament writers says about Jesus, "He learned obedience from what he suffered" (Hebrews 5:8–9). Neither obedience nor suffering is humanly attractive, but the text ought not be ignored because it presents a challenge. The writer's instruction on the connection among suffering, obedience, and salvation goes even further: "Having been perfected [through the suffering that leads to obedience], he [Jesus] became the source of eternal salvation for all who obey him."

I suggest that the key to understanding this teaching is understanding obedience as attentiveness to the reality of things, attentiveness to the properties of things, acceptance of limits in the created order of things. Jesus taught, prayed, and went about doing good. Some responded to his revelation of the mystery of God; many more resisted. Jesus accepted their reality as humans, their limited openness to new possibilities, and Jesus wept over his inability to move them—wept more than once, so the Gospel reports. Despite his suffering, he did not impose his will on them or use violence against them. His suffering was real. But he responded to his situation with respect for the mystery of human freedom and the mystery of divine grace. He faced a violent death, but he did not contribute to the violence. He was obedient to the reality of limits—his and ours. In this is our way to the salvation that he is.

### Stephanie Kaza

Some young people in Palestine are expressing profound alienation due to Israel's aggression while the world stands by doing little to help. Even young women are choosing suicide bombing as a way to transform their people's suffering. It's my own sense that these young women have broken through our stereotypes. Terrorism in this case is not just caused by aggressive, angry young men. We now see that the Palestinians are all in a desperate situation. I see this as a modern cry of abandonment.

### Zenkei Blanche Hartman

On the other hand, while the suicide bombings by young women may be acts of desperation, they may also be motivated by rage and hatred. These are the very same motivations that have led to wars throughout history. People, motivated by greed, hatred, and delusion, are always trying to control other people. This is one reason the Buddha left home to seek enlightenment.

᙭

### Father Joseph Wong

When we see the violence of terrorism, such as took place on September 11, we should not only condemn it but also engage in a thorough analysis of its cause. Some say the cause of the terrorism is hatred for America, but we need to go further and ask what causes the hatred. The terrorists' hatred may be rooted in greed and envy, or we might conclude that their actions are simply irrational.

But perhaps there are also some reasons that can make us reflect more deeply on ways we might be contributing to unjust situations in the Middle East. We may conclude that improvement in our relationship with various states in the Middle East will not occur without a change in our foreign policy, one that also supports a more equitable distribution of goods among all people of the world. A military response is not enough to deal with that deep-seated enmity and can, in fact, easily worsen the overall situation.

### Reverend Heng Sure

People come up and say: "You're a Buddhist pacifist. What do you do when a suicide bomb blows up? What do you do when a suicide bomber blows up a bus and your mother is on it, or your sister? What do Buddhists do?"

When a bomb goes off, that is like a leaf on the tip of a branch. It is the result of a process that began in a person's mind. When the bomb goes off, that is too late in the process for you to have any freedom of choice. Where the Buddha's teaching applies, where it's effective, is at the seed stage. When thoughts and feelings that can grow into violence are still seeds in your mind, you still have the freedom to plant other more powerful seeds to stop their growth. You still have a choice when you can catch the thoughts as they arise.

So, when I am insulted, when I'm beaten—when violence has been done to me and to mine—at that point I can see anger and hatred arise. These are the seeds of violence that move out of my belly and move my limbs to retaliate. If at that point I can find seeds of peace in my heart that can move me to say "It has to stop here. I do not move in anger to return violence for violence," then I have choice. Then I have freedom. Then Jesus' spirit of self-sacrifice, of turning the other cheek, is alive.

### Janet Cousins

We need to craft responses to structures of violence with structures of peace. An example of this is the University of Peace in Costa Rica, which was founded in 1981. Its motto is a turnaround of the well-known motto "If you want peace, prepare for war." Its motto is "If you want peace, prepare for peace." Its approach is to follow the words of Jesus: If you have something against your brother, try to settle it before it gets bigger and goes to court. This university and other new structures like it try to present ways of dealing with the beginnings of situations leading to violence, before they get bigger. They also provide places to converse about developing new ways to prevent violence.

### Samu Sunim

In early Buddhism, we have as a first precept *ahimsa,* nonviolence. This means not to hurt, not to do harm at any time in any situation. In Mahayana, there is an alternative for confronting aggression in certain situations: "It is better to kill one in order to save ten." If we put ourselves in the place of the Korean Buddhists who were confronted by the Japanese invasion and were seeing their families being slaughtered, perhaps we would understand this alternative better. Somehow out of their desperation, they wanted to protect their people and bring some kind of hope to those who were being victimized.

In principle I don't agree with their actions. But at least we can stretch our understanding, and in the end it's very difficult to say anything unless you have been in that situation.

🕊

### Joseph Goldstein

There is a possible source of violence identified by the Buddha that often affects religious practitioners, namely an attachment to views. A lot of religious violence comes from people who are attached to their beliefs and are intolerant of persons with other beliefs.

I had an experience of this and it was very transforming for me. Having spent twenty years in the Theravada Buddhist tradition, in the last ten years I have also been studying Tibetan Buddhism. These two tradition have different teachings and sometimes actually say quite different and opposite things about the nature of the liberated mind. Each position is presented as the truth by people I considered realized masters.

For some time, that was a tormenting *koan* for me. Who is right? It felt like my whole spiritual life depended on answering that question correctly. Then sitting with this *koan* for months, at a certain point I had what I felt was a transforming insight. It was the realization that all teachings are skillful means or methods for finding liberation. This understanding of religious views is common in many forms of Buddhism.

If we see religious teachings as skillful means, then it is

possible to be tolerant of a wide range of religious views. We can hold our own beliefs, and concerning others we can also ask the question, "How do these teachings, these views, help people to liberate their minds?" Holding our beliefs in this way keeps us from using our beliefs in ways that promote violence toward those we consider "unbelievers."

### Geshe Lobsang Tenzin

I think that there is no easy fix to the violence we find in the world today. Violence comes from many different conditions, and we need a long-term approach to it. We need to change all the conditions for violence rather than just retaliating to particular acts of violence.

Our work as spiritual guides is to address the problem within the human mind. Violence is ultimately the product of the unenlightened mind being part of an unenlightened society. As long as the mind and society are not fulfilled and at peace, delusion, greed, anger, and hatred will spill out as violence. I think that the awareness and acceptance of the fact that our minds and bodies are contaminated by certain impulses toward violence would help us not to be moved to doing violence by these impulses. Also, if we admit that these impulses are in our own minds, we can better understand how someone might be overcome by his or her own hatred and anger. This understanding can help us find more constructive and compassionate ways to respond to violence rather than just retaliating out of our own anger and hatred. Here His Holiness the Dalai Lama is a wonderful example and guide.

⚜

### Abbot John Daido Loori

When we look at the history of the human race, it is very difficult to ignore the fact that it is a history of aggression and violence. The only thing that has changed with time is our ability to invent more efficient instruments of destruction. We've become very good at it. When I think about the task of wiping out human aggression and war today, it seems like being in a leaky rowboat bailing your way across the ocean.

There is no parallel in the animal world. This morning I was watching a couple of robins compete for territory. One was singing its song. An interloper came in and they jumped around, pecked at each other, and flipped a few times. Then one flew away and there was no dead robin left behind.

On the other hand, and maybe it is because of my own stupidity, I do hold something in my heart, a feeling that there is goodness in all people. In fact, I see it all the time. And that is what keeps my hope alive when I am faced with all of the violence in our world today. My religious training also has me look at all the magnificent people who stand up and reach out. In them, I see the Buddha-nature that is in all of us.

### Ajahn Amaro

I am reminded of something that His Holiness the Dalai Lama said in a series of teachings in Los Angeles a few years ago. He was talking about nonviolence and said, "You know, if you've got a bomb, you can go into a village and you can blow up fifty people or a hundred people very easily. But if all you've got is a stick, it's really hard work to kill fifty or a hundred people. You hit a few people, you get really tired, and you have to take a rest."

What His Holiness was saying is that even though we need to look at the causes of violence, we also need to address the new technological means by which people today can exercise their violent impulses. We need to address the laws in our country that provide easy availability of firearms that can kill many people in a short amount of time with relatively little effort. His Holiness felt very strongly that religious communities should lobby for the diminution of such firearms. If we were more mindful of the huge number of deaths and injuries that are suffered each year due to children and young people having easy access to weaponry, we would be moved to do something.

### Joseph Goldstein

How do we hold the probable reality that violence will not come to an end? Would we have a different response to violence if we saw it not as something that will come to an end but as something that is ingrained in the nature of the un-awakened human condition? Somehow I feel that a certain illuminating power comes from accepting violence as an expression of the unawakened mind rather than hoping that we can bring it to an end. I wonder if by seeing it in this way, our response to violence, both internally and institutionally, would be different and perhaps more effective.

### Stephanie Kaza

Today we find ourselves in the midst of such intractable situations that at times we feel crushed by the weight of them. It seems as if the violence of the world will never go away. While it is difficult to face the suffering we feel inside us, it can be even more difficult to face the suffering we see around us. Human social structures often reflect and magnify the interpersonal tendencies that cause suffering. By examining how suffering is generated through specific thoughts, intentions, and actions of responsible parties, we can creatively transform the seeds of violence at the structural or systemic level. Liberation from suffering thus arises right in the midst of the suffering itself. Let me explore some areas of structural violence with you and offer some liberative methods from the Buddhist tradition that might be useful.

The types of suffering that derive from military aggression

are plain to see and painful to witness. Social infrastructures literally crumble when bombs and guns destroy families, homes, communities, utilities, and government offices. Military spending for arms, soldiers, fuel, and transport drains economic resources from social welfare needs such as health care and education, adding to the downward spiral of war-torn communities. The United States is the world's leading exporter of arms, supplying over $700 billion worth of arms to over fifty authoritarian governments. Traditional Buddhist liberative methods appropriate to this suffering include *ahimsa,* or non-harming, and the bodhisattva vow to liberate all beings from suffering.

Think of the types of suffering that result from racism, classism, and sexism: job inequity and insecurity, exposure to workplace hazards, physical and emotional abuse, and psychological violence of shame, alienation, and marginalization from society. While personal stereotyping can hurt individual feelings, structural discrimination often causes far greater damage across whole populations of those designated as inferior. Transforming conditioned values and worldviews so deeply embedded in social structures is extremely difficult. Zen Buddhism in particular emphasizes the method of cultivating nondualistic mind, seeing the self and other as cocreated and cocreating.

Much environmental suffering stems from mechanistic, utilitarian views of nature as well as reductionist short-term thinking. Clear-cutting, destruction of habitat, species extinctions, air and water pollution—collectively these have caused tremendous ecosystem violence, to the point that human health and stability are threatened worldwide. The Buddhist law of interdependence can be helpful in analyzing the multicausal nature of existence, emphasizing the relationality of beings more than their separate "thingness." The law of karma is also important in studying the ecological consequences of present actions for future generations.

Suffering of cultural consciousness is strongly influenced by media violence. People young and old are exposed to violence in advertising and programs twenty-four hours a day. Many households have three or four televisions; children spend more time watching television than any other activity except sleeping. Escalation of violence in TV dramas implants suggestions in viewers' minds that may be acted out off screen. Advertising deliberately generates dissatisfaction and desire for material goods, often using violent images to sell products. Buddhist teacher Thich Nhat Hanh has suggested that the Fifth Precept on avoiding intoxication be applied to the media and other modern consciousness-polluting influences. Buddhist retreat centers often serve as detox zones for those overwhelmed by the speed and overstimulation of media-society.

Human suffering also takes structural form in the widespread abuse of workers. The current Western focus on material possessions has emphasized economic values over spiritual and social values. Manufacturers outsource their assembly-line needs, going overseas for cheap labor. Free trade agreements help promote inhumane labor conditions; desire for American goods escalates global appetites for more and more products, accelerating poor treatment of workers. Buddhists committed to transforming the culture of materialism can share practices of restraint and simplicity that have been the hallmark of monastic practice for centuries. Teachings on attachment, desire, ignorance, and dependent origination are all very useful in cutting the root of desire for material goods.

Structural levels of suffering can be much more intractable and difficult to transform than individual relations. Religious leaders and institutions have always been powerful social forces influencing other major systems players. Facing the structural problems of our world as an individual is not as powerful as facing them through institutional action. The pope, for example, can speak to presidents and others heads of state representing the entire Catholic Church. The depth and scale of the structural concerns suggest it is time for religious leaders to take up positions as institutional players and work their liberative methods on the big scale. Though we may not yet have the necessary skillful means, the very problems call so loudly for our attention that they will point the way to effective action.

### Father Daniel Ward

I do believe we need to look at the violence in the world and our society, but I also think we need to look at our own institutions, our own religious structures, our own teachings. We need to ask ourselves: How are they contributing to violence?

As an old song in the Catholic Church goes, "Peace, let it begin with me." Since the issues of violence are systemic, we must begin with the systemic problems in our own institutions.

This is difficult for us to do because it's always easier, whether we are an individual or an institution, to talk about "out there." The hardest thing, and we see this in the Catholic Church today, is to talk about ourselves and our own problems and how we contribute to the issues of violence and suffering. But if we do, I think that we find that hatred is not the only source of violence, structurally speaking.

A basic issue behind structural violence is probably patriarchy. It often seems that patriarchal structures dominate within our institutions, in systems of exclusion and control, divinizing teachings and structures that are really time based and gender based. We can see this in other religions as well. Rita M. Gross has written a wonderful book, *Buddhism after Patriarchy,* on this topic in the Buddhist context.

As a good law professor, I don't have the answers, but what I do have are some questions about institutional structures that I think we should all take to heart no matter what our religion may be. So, my first question is: How do patriarchal structures dominate within our institutions, in structures of domination and control, systems of exclusion, practices of ownership of land and creatures and things, divinizing teachings and structures that are really time based and gender based?

My second question is: How many of our structures and systems and teachings alienate? For instance, systems or teachings that create barriers of righteousness and divisions, teachings or attitudes that cause competition or a need to appear better, more correct, or have the better way or the better teaching?

A third question is: Has the institution, the system, the teaching, become more important than the people within and outside of them? Has the religious institution or system become more important than the journey of the seekers?

Fourth: Has the religious institution or system become so dominant and important as to destroy the harmony of creation? What need we change in our structures, systems, or teachings so that, as microcosms of our world, we are transforming institutions, ones that hold out not only a way but also a hope and a reality to the rest of our world?

I believe many of the issues facing the Catholic Church today are caused by a refusal to ask and seek answers to questions because the institution has become more important. It is necessary for people in the church who are in pain to be able to speak and be heard. Those who come to us need to feel cared for as they lift up their pain. Recall Benedict's teaching: The one who is the spiritual guide for the seeker ought never crush the bruised reed.

### Paul Gailey

For many years I held a position in an institution where I had a great deal of authority. Then I went to a position in another organization where I had very little authority. This experience was a great gift because from the bottom I could see certain things that were difficult to see from the top. Within the group in power, there is a great deal of self-containment. In other words, it's very easy for those in authority to justify all the reasons why they need what they say they need within the institution and to blind themselves to the subtle ways that their actions are affecting others. We can see how this kind of thinking has recently played itself out so tragically in the corporate world. As I've watched groups that have worked in this way, I've come to see that much of this behavior comes from fear, from fear of losing what people feel they need. But it's extremely difficult for those in positions of power to see this.

***

### Father Leo Lefebure

A few years ago, before the year 2000, Pope John Paul II challenged Catholics to prepare for the third millennium of Christian faith through a purification of memory, acknowledging that terrible things had been done by Catholics in the name of Christ and asking God's forgiveness so we could move forward. I think that challenge probably goes even deeper and broader than the pope himself ever intended.

On one hand, there have been some dramatic signs of progress. Probably the most dramatic hopeful sign was when the pope went to Jerusalem and put a prayer into the Western Wall, the most sacred site for Jews, asking forgiveness for the terrible sins of Catholics against Jews. This goes right to the very central moments and symbols of the Catholic tradition. The crucifixion was for centuries used as a weapon to beat up Jews. Our own Scriptures, as traditionally understood, feed right into this. Part of the necessary purification of memory goes right to the most central moment of our faith. This is an example of where we've become quite willing to be honest and talk.

But having said this, on a number of other more internal issues, there are limits on what we are permitted to discuss—for example, women's issues. The culture of dialogue that the pope has called for is often easier to carry out when Catholics talk with Buddhists than it is when we would like to talk internally about a whole nexus of issues. This is a tremendous tragedy.

### Prioress Mary Collins

I think there is another level to the problem of authority in the church, which at least those of us who aren't part of it can recognize, and that is clerical culture. There is a subculture within the Catholic Church that is distinctive, and it carries a lot of unexamined assumptions and presuppositions. I'm not sure seminaries are dealing with this, nor do I think monasteries are dealing with the bias and the burden that is on the rest of the church.

For those of you who are not familiar with clerical culture, it has to do with an experience of exclusion of women and of women's sensibilities and sensitivities. I experienced it in the summer of 1976, when I was at St. John's Abbey. At that time there was a growing awareness of women's concerns about language, so the women who were there wanted to get students and faculty into this conversation. In fact, what we got instead was retaliation, very childish, from the young man who was at that time one of the monks involved in leading music. He started choosing all the hymns that he could find that spoke exclusively to men in the church.

It was a very childish response, but it was also a refusal to listen with the heart to really hear the pain of women. This refusal came from the position of institutional power that says "We are in charge here. We don't have to listen to you, and we don't have to attend to you."

I think that much of what's happening right now in priestly formation in seminaries is still an attempt to maintain the clerical culture. It's talked about in terms of maintaining priestly identity, but I think priestly identity becomes identified with clerical culture. It's very hierarchical, a patronage system that is built on ascending to positions of power. The assumption is that if you are associated with the right people and do the right things, then the time will come when you receive more and more power in the institution.

Certainly there are ordained priests who choose not to participate in this system, but to the degree that they don't, they remain nobodies in the system. Also, there are bishops who have tried to block the clerical culture, but they become bishops of Small Town Nowhere and stay there the rest of their lives because they have not participated.

### Father William Skudlarek

Clerical culture is a culture of power, privilege, and exclusion. It comes by virtue of being ordained, being male, being obedient, not questioning authority, doing what you are told, and not asking questions that you are told not to ask.

### Father Donald Grabner

At the Second Vatican Council, I think it was the Belgian Cardinal de Smedt who got up and said that the three major problems that the church faces are triumphalism, juridicalism, and clericalism. Clericalism has its temptations because the rewards it gives to those who play the game are significant. While many priests do not choose to play and are wonderful pastors and people, a number of clerics are giving in to those temptations. The abuse of authority and other painful issues in the church are aggravated by clericalism.

### Father Kevin Hunt

I've been in the monastery forty-eight years now, and for about the first twenty-five of those years I was a lay brother. For those who don't know the distinction within the Christian monastic community, at that time there were clerics, also called choir monks, and there were lay brothers. The lay brothers were traditionally considered the servants of the monastery, the ones who did the basic manual labor.

I found during those years—and still find because I'm not somebody in authority in my community—that I was best able to identify who I was when an old black man told me, "You know, you are the nonexistent person in a community." He was talking about how people look around and automatically their eyes jump over you. I think there are people like this in every community, in every social reality. We tend to call them the marginalized.

How are we going to confront the issue of those who exist in our communities but are nonexistent, no matter what the reason: whether it's because they are gay, lay brothers, or women, or because of their race, their lack of education, or their type of education?

### Ajahn Amaro

The Buddhist world is not exempt from problematic relationships between men and women in the religious life. Full ordination for women in the Buddhist monastic order is a major, major issue these days. Like many of my Catholic brothers, I did not become a monk in order to subjugate women. But I became part of an institution with its own history.

❧

### Venerable Thubten Chodron

There are levels of ordination in Buddhism: novice and full ordination. To become a fully ordained nun, one needs to be ordained by a group of fully ordained nuns and fully ordained monks. However, there are provisions in the *Vinaya*—our code of monastic discipline—where just men can ordain women.

It is also very important that the lineage of ordination be traced back to the Buddha. The lineage of full ordination for women did not spread to Tibet or to Thailand. It spread to Sri Lanka, but it was wiped out during a war centuries ago. It also spread to Korea, Vietnam, and China, and continues to exist in East Asia today.

Some women, from traditions where full ordination does not exist for them, are considering the possibility of full ordination in East Asia. This is creating a lot of waves in the system. The waves are always phrased in terms of doctrine—to make sure that the lineage can be traced back to the time of the Buddha and that all the detailed procedural parts have been kept intact over the centuries. The people making this determination of whether to accept full ordination for nuns in countries where it is currently not present are the male monastics. For them, the discussion is ostensibly about *Vinaya* legalities.

But I think there are other issues involved. It may hurt the pride of one tradition to accept a lineage from another. Also, fully ordained women would be more independent. Right now, nuns are not abbesses of their own nunneries in Tibet. A monk is always the abbot of a nunnery. If women become fully ordained, they would take charge of their own nunneries, train their own nuns, and become more active and better educated. The laypeople would respect them and give more donations to them. This would change the old social structure dramatically.

These kinds of issues are not getting addressed because in the structure of religious institutions, we are taught not to ask certain questions out of respect for our teachers—who are male. When you start to ask them, you get certain looks.

### Ajahn Sundara

We do not have high or full ordination in our Theravada tradition. It died out some eleven hundred years ago. There is an interest among some monks of our tradition to help revive the fully ordained women's order. However, the institution makes it quite difficult to get things started, even though one might think it is the right time. But there has to be a common agreement among the elders, and that could take some time. To reestablish this ancient order of nuns would be a momentous event.

For nuns in our community, there is not a burning desire to become fully ordained, even though there is a definite sense that it will be an important step. Our interest is more focused on liberating the heart. That is really the forefront of our daily life. It is more important than anything else.

### Geshe Lobsang Tenzin

The question about the full ordination of nuns is very much rooted in our cultural ideas about male and female roles. There is no justification for not having full ordination for nuns in the Tibetan tradition. His Holiness the Dalai Lama certainly has recognized this fact. He has taken the initiative to have the monastic elders find ways that the women's ordination lineage can be transmitted. The decision about this important matter needs to be a communal one, but the old culture with its definition of gender roles is hard to change.

### Venerable Henepola Gunaratana

I myself have ordained several women, and one of them even received full ordination according to the Chinese tradition. I participated in one ceremony in Taiwan where Theravada women novices took full ordination and then went back to their own countries, especially Sri Lanka, and received another full ordination from monks. Now, as to the question of its legitimacy, there is no stipulation in the *Vinaya* that once the order is dead, it should not be revived. It is only the male-dominated *Sangha* (monastic community) that upholds the view that it should not be revived.

### Venerable Thubten Chodron

I was thinking about the quote from His Holiness the Dalai Lama, that violence is any action motivated by hatred. That is definitely true, and we need to be more aware of that fact. Hatred has subtle nuances. For example, arrogance may not look like hatred, but it places oneself above others in a way that does violence to others' dignity as persons. One may not feel hatred toward others, but one's arrogance may make one less caring about others so that one may even allow them to be harmed in violent ways. Hatred may not be blazing forth in one's arrogant lack of caring, but it still produces violence.

I see this happening in the recent sexual abuse scandals in the Catholic Church. Now, I say this as a Buddhist who knows that we too have had a number of serious scandals in which people have been abused. It seems that when our religious institutions fall into abuse, it is because of arrogance and a lack of caring for others. One cares more for protecting the institution than protecting those who are victimized by the institution. We religious people need to come up with a response to the problem of arrogance in order to heal our houses.

### Father Daniel Ward

Concerning the sexual abuse scandal, for us it is not merely a scandal in the newspaper. It is a real tragedy that happens to real people. In facing this tragedy in our own community, we have found that when you admit the shame, you don't have to worry that it's going to kill the institution. You can't act as if the only reason for existence is to keep the institution going.

Another important thing was that we brought therapists in and had community discussions, allowing people to say freely how they felt. Also, in working as a lawyer with victims, I remember a young man who, when all the discussions leading up to a settlement had been finished, all of a sudden just shouted out: "All my years of pain and this is all it is, money?" From that point on, I always insisted that when I went to a settlement conference, part of the settlement had to be a meeting of the victim and the abuser. The abuser had to be able to listen to the pain that was caused. He had to face the shame. This, I think, is the progress we have made as a community, as an institution, but it is something we still have to deal with.

𝓦

### Geshe Lhundub Sopa

All people have difficulties when their sexuality dominates their minds and bodies. These difficulties exist in religious institutions just like everywhere else. When sexual misconduct happens in a religious institutional setting, the common reaction is to keep it secret. But when this happens, the result is unhealthy. On the other hand, when the problem becomes public and has to be dealt with by the institution, the result can be purifying. It may be painful at first, but the result of the purification will be a greater health in the community.

It is very difficult to stop sexual misconduct right away. Sexuality is the cause of a dominating attachment to other persons. So it is important to become more clearly aware of the consequences of sexual misbehavior: the shamefulness of it, the pain that it brings to self and others, the loss of self-respect and the respect of others. One should also become more aware of the benefits of chastity such as freedom from dominating attachments and growth in the spiritual life.

𝓦

### Lama Eric Marcoux

First of all, do hear my emotion. As a therapist, I have been involved in the field of working with sexual misbehavior for about seventeen years. I am retired now, mostly because I am tired of the pain.

I have seen the other side. I have seen into the painful lives of people who, to compensate for their humiliating and irresponsible lapses, have managed to be perhaps better than I have ever been.

From a Buddhist point of view, consequences are the result of many causes and conditions. I would suggest that a structure of internalized sexual violence against oneself and others comes from unresolved childhood and adult curiosities about sexuality as well as deeply wounding and scarring personal deprivation.

If we let our minds rest on the humanity of the perpetrators of sexual misconduct—perhaps visualizing, for example, a priest at the altar grieving and ashamed the morning after an inappropriate behavior—we can, for a moment, look beyond their actions and the sickness that motivated them. We can see that these are real people, people with families, people with a profound love of God and the ability to serve and care for others in ways that are truly inspiring. Professionally, I have felt their sadness, their fear, their remorse, their honest guilt and shame. And I think everyone knows what that is like.

### Father Thomas Baima

The church in the United States has taken some strong and decisive steps to deal with the sexual abuse scandal. I would like to share something about how the institution that I serve in, Mundelein Seminary, has dealt with this painful situation. Seminaries have been somewhat at the forefront of the story because, of course, we are the ones that train priests. We've done four things in response to the scandal. First, the rector of the seminary called the entire seminary community together—both the faculty and the students—for an open forum. There was an open microphone so people could really raise any question that they had.

The principal concern was for the students, who are feeling the brunt of this scandal because they are in the process of discerning their vocation to the priesthood. This places a tremendous burden on them, both as members of the church and as young men who are preparing to assume this role within the church. They had many questions: What is the church doing? What is really happening?

We have a certain advantage in that the rector of our seminary was previously the vicar for priests in the Archdiocese of Chicago. The vicar is the priest who is especially appointed by the bishop to handle problem cases in personnel. As it happened, Father John Canary, who is our rector, was the vicar for priests at the time in the early 1990s when the Archdiocese of Chicago went through its own struggles with some scandals. Out of that experience came a whole new approach led by Cardinal Bernardin. It aimed first of all at protecting children, second at respecting the victims and ministering to them, and third at ministering to the clergy who had been involved. Father Canary was therefore able to explain these policies, their genesis, and how they had been played out in Chicago since then. There was somewhat lively discussion from the students afterward.

The second thing we did resulted from an oversight: We had invited the faculty and students but had forgotten the staff of the university. These are the folks—the secretaries, the professional workers, the grounds crew—all those who were suddenly taken to be official spokespersons of the church. Their friends would be coming up to them in social gatherings and saying: "You work for the seminary. What's this all about?" They were feeling an enormous pressure, so we repeated the open forum with the full body of staff.

The third thing that we did is related to our monthly gathering for a community Mass to pray for special needs. Originally it was begun to pray for the situation in our country after September 11, but it gradually became a time of intercession for whatever burdens people were carrying. We continued that event all year, so that it became a place where people could come together and pray about all these situations, the scandal included. The daily liturgies for the seminarians served in the same way.

Another thing that we did, which we felt was important, was speak to the wider community. We had been receiving enormous numbers of requests from the news media to talk about how seminaries had changed since thirty years ago. Father Canary made the determination that it would probably be of benefit to the wider community if we did a comprehensive piece on seminary formation, particularly on how it has changed. This meant the recruitment, the selection process, the training and evaluation of candidates preparing for the priesthood. So we allowed the *New York Times* to send a reporter and set up approximately twenty-five interviews, giving her pretty much unrestricted access to the faculty and administration. This was a transparent way of saying that the situation now is radically different than it was thirty years ago.

Much to my surprise, the *Times* piece was the lead article, the headline. We've all had some bad experiences with the media, but I'd have to say the article was so well written that I wouldn't have changed a word of it. The reporter obviously was pretty smart, had listened carefully, and had done a professional job of telling the story. We were very, very grateful for that.

The really remarkable thing was the many thankful phone calls that came after that from people across the country who had read the article. We are all dealing with our anger over the situation, our sorrow, our deep sense of embarrassment and shame that this has happened. But I'm confident that we will work through this, provided we continue to talk about it and not throw the cloak of invisibility over the elephant in the very center of the church's room.

# CHAPTER TEN

# Accepting Sickness and Aging

## FROM RESISTANCE TO LETTING GO

*Father Donald Grabner*
Every event in the Christian's life is to be viewed and evaluated in the light of his or her participation in the mystery of Christ's passover from death to life. Nevertheless, it is our experience of what Teilhard de Chardin called the "diminishments" of life that seems most quickly to catch our attention. These diminishments, these aspects of our existence that form what he called "the darkest element and the most despairingly useless years of our

life," seem to confront us with a great practical opportunity to translate our faith into a conscious and active response to God's will for us individually.

Principal among these diminishments are illness and aging, which in one way or another are the lot of all human beings. All of us inevitably encounter these innate and challenging characteristics of humanity, both in others and in ourselves. They forcefully call our attention to our finiteness, our transitoriness. The numerous, often close-knit relations that unite the members of the monastic community are a special witness to the resurrection-faith that confronts these issues head-on. To foster these relations, we are constantly encouraged by Benedict to bear patiently with one another both the infirmities of mind and body and the weaknesses of old age. These are ever-present reminders that the Christian transformation from death to life is a process, reminders that we begin to die the day we are born. We are daily reminded that we are working together in community toward the culmination of that process throughout our whole earthly existence.

As I learned early on when I was a novice, Benedict makes a very practical application of these reflections in his chapters on the care of the sick in the monastery and on the care of the elderly and the young. Thus he states in chapter 36 of the *Rule*:

> *The care of those who are sick in the community is an absolute priority which must rank before every other requirement so that there may be no doubt that it is Christ who is truly served in them. After all, Christ said "I was sick and you came to visit*

*me,"* and also, *"What you did to one of these least brethren you did to me."*

Learning to accept the frailties of another, therefore, is perceived by Benedict as a useful means for one's own growth in that love which is the essence of the Christian life.

For this reason, when we were novices and then newly professed monks, our novice master and cleric master would regularly assign us to cleaning tasks in the infirmary. There, of necessity, we came into greater contact with the infirm and the elderly of the community. This, in a special way, involved those confreres whose weaknesses had reached such a stage that special attention had to be given to their care. In addition, whenever some monk needs to be taken to the nearby St. Francis Hospital in the town of Maryville because of some severe illness, all the monks who possibly can take turns staying with him, especially if death seems imminent. The communal dimension of monastic life is wonderfully manifested in these instances of care for the weak and the elderly. It is a clear witness to everyone as to the value of all human life.

### Ajahn Sundara

I would like to ask you to just close your eyes gently, or just sit quietly and bring into your heart a time in your life when you were either sick or experiencing the beginning of losing your identity as a vigorous, useful human being with a great sense of belonging to life, family, and community. Can you remember the feelings that came up when you suddenly felt those changes taking place in yourself? Can you remember how you felt as you became limited physically or mentally, as your vigor and your mind were not so powerful?

Perhaps you can also remember how you were affected by the way people saw you as you were getting older or were stricken by an illness of some kind. What did you feel like in your heart? How was your thinking about yourself connected with that experience? What kind of emotion was predominant at the time: doubt, fear? How was your future seen from that experience of illness and aging?

As a human being, what is important is how we deal with experiences such as sickness and aging. From a Buddhist perspective, those experiences provide us with particular contexts in which we can free our minds. Freeing the mind through those experiences means allowing everything that arises in the midst of those experiences to be made completely conscious and to be accepted fully.

About seven years after I became a nun, two elderly women, who had been Buddhists for much of their lives, were invited by my teacher to end their days at our monastery. At the time, the nuns were rather young, vigorous and in good health. We were the bouncy, energetic type, and we did not have a clue what older people were like. I was trained as a dancer myself, and anybody who didn't look like a dancer looked sort of crippled! Elderly people had never entered in my life until these women turned up. I had met older people, but I really did not see them.

One woman had moments of paranoia, and the other, who had been a Buddhist scholar, was slowly losing her mind. She suffered from Alzheimer's. So, having those two elderly women in the midst of our community was an extraordinary learning experience. They slowed us down. They made us extremely patient. They drove us crazy. And we had a lot of fun.

What did we learn? The lessons came through realizing how much we value things like health, youth, physical and psychological comforts. Given our modern obsession with youth and health, sickness and aging are most often seen as anomalies. We feel that they should not be part of the normal cycle of human life. I think until we are sick, until we are getting older, we do not fully realize the amount of resistance there is in our heart to the natural unfolding of this human body. This resistance can lead us to buy or do things that will keep us looking young and pretty. But what happens to the heart when we pursue this ideal? What does it feel like to pretend that we are still something we are not?

Since that experience with our elderly guests, one thing that has struck me during my travels is that most traditional cultures around the world honor the full cycle of human life. There are even ceremonies and particular preparations to enter the different stages of one's life. But in our country, there are so many products that lead us to believe that we will stay young forever that we never learn to move through these passages of our lives with any sense of grace and meaning. I think that the reason for this resistance is fear. We don't want to lose control. We are terrified at the possibility of being "set aside" by our family, friends, or community due to illness or aging. Our consumer culture reinforces this fear by considering older people to be helpless and useless. This is really sad.

On the other hand, old age is a challenge. The Buddha described it in these words:

> *Have not you seen a woman or a man, age eighty, ninety or a hundred years, frail, bent like a roof bracket, crooked, leaning on a stick, shakily going along, ailing, youth and vigor gone, with broken teeth, with gray and scanty hair or none at all, wrinkled with blotched limbs?*

Certainly with no inner resources to cope with this kind of deterioration of our body and our mind, we can become quite miserable and bitter. How many older people live in a prison of resentment and anger with no buoyancy in their heart and no sense of the beauty of their humanness? But then we also find older people who have chosen another way of living their latter years by realizing the inevitability of their conditions with a sense of empathy and peace. What makes some people face their sickness or aging with fear and bitterness, and others with compassion and acceptance?

If we did not try to avoid the latter stages of the cycle of human living, we would find in them important lessons about the meaning of life itself. We could read the meaning of life in our bodies as we contemplate the changes we are undergoing. Without being unrealistically poetic, we can take our sickness or aging into our hearts and find a deeper acceptance of our life. In this way, the tone of our fear changes. We find an openness to life, to its fragility, and to others who are also in need of help or understanding.

For any of us who have practiced the spiritual life, either meditation or prayer, I think we all discover that there is a process of transformation that arises through abiding totally with difficult or painful experiences. To run away from the difficulties or the pain leaves the possible transformation behind, as well. In a spiritual path, one advances as one looks more and more deeply to see the truth about our life as it really is, not how we would want it to be.

It has always amazed me how people who were sick discovered through their sickness a strength and a courage that they never thought they had, a kind of resilience of the spirit. It is at the time of sickness and aging that many of us give ourselves, perhaps for the very first time, the permission to simply be. Those times can give us an extraordinary space inwardly and outwardly to find a new and transformative level of self-acceptance and peace, of accepting our whole life from beginning to end.

I knew a woman who was dying of cancer. Through her mindfulness and patience with herself, she deepened her insight into the truth about suffering in a way that made her a more loving person. She made peace with her illness in a way that enabled her to appreciate the preciousness of life. She said that her experience with cancer clarified her priorities and led her to discover that real happiness is found inside, in a more peaceful and contented mind full of compassion, generosity, and selflessness. Her transformation was a blessing to all who met her.

꙲

### Prioress Margaret Michaud

Our culture tends to deny the fact of aging. Youth and health are somehow to be held on to forever. When people of our times are forced to confront the reality of aging, it is usually with a profound sense of loathing and disgust. For many, aging means a forced retreat from active life. The old are shoved to the sidelines of the modern arena. Their opinions are often seen as outdated, irrelevant, and useless. Our Western culture, with its fixation on youth, speed, and convenience, has no time for those whose lives have necessarily slowed down. These folks cannot move as fast or think as quickly as they once could. Their physical limitations can make getting around a chore. Events of the past may seem more real to them than today's happenings. There are those among the young who have no patience hearing talk of "the old days."

We can helpfully look to the *Rule* of Benedict for advice in relating to the elderly. In chapter 37, "The Elderly and Children," we read that these groups "should be treated with kindly consideration." Both groups are in a state of weakness in comparison with the energy of young and middle-age adults. The consideration that Benedict asks for does not, as he points out in the same chapter, derive merely from a natural or spontaneous tendency. It is the fruit of thoughtful and prayerful reflection on the presence of God in all persons. In regard to the elderly, compassion may be a challenge in dealing with those who have not aged gracefully but who are difficult and thus create friction between their generation and the young. Nevertheless, the practice in monasteries that follow Benedict's *Rule* has always been to treat the aged members of the community with gentle consideration, quality care, and genuine love. This is a major way in which the monastery gives witness to the blessedness of life.

### Venerable Henepola Gunaratana

In some societies, a child is born in the center of a circle of attention. Everybody pays attention to the center. As the child grows up, that circle grows bigger and bigger and bigger, especially as the individual becomes a productive member of society. Everybody acknowledges the person and recognizes his or her contributions.

But when productivity decreases with aging, then people withdraw their attention, their recognition and appreciation. Eventually the person find himself or herself at the periphery of the circle. When a person is very, very old, he or she goes out of the circle into a senior citizens' home. It may be very close to the funeral home. Nobody wants to look at the person, let alone attend his or her needs. We hire people to do this chore.

In other societies, the older the person, the greater the respect. Younger people are taught to respect the elderly. But in our capitalistic society, one's value is measured in terms of productivity and consumption. And in our materialistic society, youth is worshiped and aging is seen as a process of losing value. We need to discover the value of all living beings at all stages of the life cycle. We need to see people of all ages with the eyes of acceptance and the heart of compassion. And we need to begin to do this with ourselves.

### Father Columba Stewart

For all of our Christian assertions that we are made in the image and likeness of God and that we are destined for eternal life with the triune God, the fact of human mortality creeps over and through all that we do. Dealing with mortality is perhaps the greatest existential challenge facing every human being. Whether denied or accepted, fought or embraced, the narrowing of possibilities in this life is one of our inevitable asceticisms.

The ache of mortality can drive us in opposite directions. On one hand, we can react by resistance and denial. We can behave as if seizing control of the minutiae of our lives will allow us, by some fallacious analogy, to manage the big picture also. This illusion of mastery pushes us into isolation, both from our own deeper longings and from other people. We find ourselves uttering the pseudo-Stoicisms of "I can handle it," or "No, no, I'm fine, really," or "It would be easier to do it myself." When I hear or say such things, it is a danger signal.

Fear of mortality can also push us in the opposite direction, into illusory attachments. We think that acquisition of people, things, or experiences will compensate for the slow evaporation of all that we know of this life. The assumption that we can fill the holes in our hearts through acquisition and possession is the very foundation of the consumer economy of the Western world. We know that the lies of consumerism are built on the exploitation of the poor. We know that marketing is manipulation of our uneasiness with accepting life as it is, unpredictable and transitory. Nonetheless, the urge to possess, even at the expense of others in greater need, arises deep within the human psyche. We fight to get what we want, from the tussles on playgrounds to the global horrors of imperialism.

The success of Christianity in its first fervor had largely to do with its promise of an ultimate resolution of the pain of transitory existence through a resurrection of the body and everlasting life. There has never, however, been any assurance from Christian teachers that the sting of mortality vanishes when one is baptized or receives the Eucharist or is faithful to spiritual practices. The irony is that dedication to prayer makes the anguish more acute even as it opens new perspectives on the human situation. Because we typically use physical or psychological painkillers to dull the ache of mortality, real commitment to prayer opens up emotional and spiritual systems that usually are underdeveloped or repressed in the arbitrage we employ to get through life.

But life is meant to be lived, not simply survived, and one of the vital lessons in learning to live is accepting that we will die. Benedict lists the practice of "keeping death daily before our eyes" as one of his "tools for good works." This was not a macabre obsession with death but a frank acknowledgment of the contingency of life and the inestimable value of each day as an opportunity for conversion.

### Venerable Henepola Gunaratana

Until I was twenty years old, I had a photographic memory. I was able to read hundreds of pages in a book in a matter of minutes and remembered everything. If somebody asked me a question about what I had read, I was able to answer giving the page numbers and even the punctuation marks. Everything stuck in my mind. Then, at the age of twenty, I had amnesia and I lost my memory so badly that I could not recognize the alphabet.

I was always proud of myself because of my memory. When I lost my memory, I was desperate; it was just like poking a hole in a big balloon with a pin. My pride disappeared, and I was so desperate that I wanted to commit suicide. But in the end, this sickness brought about a major transformation of my life. It brought me down to earth, to finding an identity with others on an equal basis. By finally accepting myself with my limitations, I could better accept others with theirs.

Another time I also faced death. In 1976 I was flying out to Sri Lanka from Hawaii. I was sitting in a window seat. About an hour after taking off, I saw fire coming from one of the engines. The next minute the pilot announced that that engine was on fire, and the flight attendants began to explain how to deplane if we made it back to Hawaii. Meanwhile, I was watching the fire that was sometimes blue, sometimes yellow, and sometimes red. Then I turned around and looked at the people on the airplane. Except for the tiny children, everybody was deathly fear-stricken. Some were crying. Some were kissing. Some were hugging. Some were almost half dead.

This is not meant for boasting, but since I had learned to face death in my meditation practice, I remained mindful. Every night, even now, when I go to bed I reflect, "This is my last night. Tomorrow I will not wake up." When I wake up, I live with the awareness that every moment I'm dying. So on the airplane I thought: "This is the moment that I'm going to die." And I was able to be at peace.

Of course, our plane managed to get back to Hawaii. The chutes came down, and we all jumped on them. That was the first time in my life I slid down a chute. Even as a little child, I never slid down a slide. So the chute was great fun!

### Sister Barbara McCracken

For some years I've had on a little card on my desk that line from the *Rule* of Benedict about keeping death daily before your eyes. A few months ago I did have a serious illness, and I tried to examine all the feelings that came up within me when I found out that I was so very ill. I probably didn't handle some of the feelings too well, but the main thing I discovered was that I had felt a loss of control. When I asked myself what I really control in my life, I finally decided it was just my calendar, my book with all my appointments in it and all of the activities in which I am involved. Faced with death, I could finally let go of my scheduling of my life, my attempts to control my life. Then I found a much deeper sense of gratitude for my life, whatever it may bring. Right now my medical prognosis is pretty good, but I certainly don't want to go back to the way of living as I had in the past.

### Ajahn Sundara

Two statements in our tradition present a kind of paradox. The first one, in the words of the Buddha, is "Whatever arises is suffering; and whatever passes away is suffering." The other statement is that suffering can lead to the increase of suffering, or suffering can lead to the decrease of suffering.

The first statement defines our human condition. The second statement indicates what we can do with that condition in the context of practice. In practice, we learn not to grasp the suffering, and that in itself leads to a kind of letting go of suffering. In this letting go, the suffering decreases. If we cling to it, the suffering gets worse. For example, if I cling to concepts that judge my illness as bad, a terrible waste of my life, and so on, those thoughts increase my suffering. By an acceptance of the illness just as it is, not making it worse by worry or judgment, my suffering decreases.

### Father Julian von Duerbeck

Some years ago one of our brothers was in a major clinical depression; he really wanted to die. The interior suffering was so great, he said, that he planned suicides. A number of times he had the blade right at his jugular. What stopped him each time? He told me that it was not fear of hell, because he does not believe that God condemns suicides, but he would think about saying good-bye to the people that he loved. That is what stopped him. He knew that we, from whom he had so well hidden these thoughts and plans, would blame ourselves. We would look back over our lives and say, "When did I miss this, to let him go ahead with this?"

After some time he accepted his condition and did find the help he needed. When he got better, he shared that he owed his way of thinking about the nature and value of friendship to a monastic writer, St. Aelred of Rievaulx, and his treatise

*Spiritual Friendship.* This sense of being spiritually connected to others, of not just being a single individual, offered him hope in the midst of the darkness. And, of course, St. Aelred's whole theology of spiritual friendship centers on Jesus at the Last Supper where he embraces us as friends.

### Zenkei Blanche Hartman

I have had a heart attack, and I nearly died. Sometime later I developed the attitude that "Okay, I'll die of a heart attack some day. I can accept that." But then I developed atrial fibrillation, and one of the risks of atrial fibrillation is stroke. I noticed that I was much more afraid of being disabled, dependent, and not being able to communicate than I was about dying. I think it is easier for us to accept death than being incapacitated.

When I came down with atrial fibrillation, I found that I didn't have the stamina that I was accustomed to having. There were some days when I felt I really should not get up to open the *Zendo,* or meditation hall, and do the morning service. But I was the abbess; so I would get up anyhow. Then, a couple of hours later, I would have a fibrillation and would have to go to bed for twenty-four hours for it to go away. I thought, "Well, maybe I'm going to have to resign." I was feeling terrible about my condition.

One day I said to my friend, "I cannot get up every morning. So I'm going to have to resign as abbess." And she replied, "No, you don't." I responded, "Well, Suzuki Roshi got up every morning." And she said, "No, he didn't. Don't you remember when he got sick and told us that we might have to sit *zazen* for him some days if he were not here?"

When I heard this, I realized that I had an idea of myself as the "heroic abbess" leading her community! So the next time I gave a Dharma talk, I told my community about my medical problem. I told them the truth, that I might not be able to open the *Zendo* some mornings. Once I took that pressure off myself, I never had another incident like that.

꙰

### Father Joseph Wong

I would like to share a story about the transforming power of suffering caused by sickness. Brother Philip, who died in 1995 at the age of eighty-eight, is now a kind of legend in our community. Of German descent, he was very tough and earnest in his monastic life, conservative in his faith, strict in his monastic observance, and very demanding toward himself and toward others. He would often challenge members of the community who did not live up to his standards, so he was a kind of terror to the community.

The gradual change began to take place when in his late seventies he was diagnosed with colon cancer and had to undergo a surgery. As a consequence he needed to wear a colostomy bag and was much weakened in his activities. Then sometime after he had turned eighty, he was brought to a veterans' hospital and kept there for two months because of constant diarrhea. When he was released from the hospital the doctor gave him only a short time to live—which turned out to be eight long years! He was unable to walk and had to be moved around in a wheelchair. Each day a monk was assigned to look after him. With the loss of mobility he felt that he had lost control of his life and was completely in the hands of others. This was cause of great suffering for him but also cause of special grace.

There was yet another challenge, or blessing, awaiting him. A nurse at the veterans' hospital, Mariellen, who had taken care of him while he was there, volunteered to come to our Hermitage on weekends to offer him special service. She was a robust woman in her late forties. She was loving and caring but felt that she should be in command of the situation. She was firm in her dealings with the patient, whether it concerned the schedule, the way of taking medicine, or whatever. The two strong personalities clashed continually at the beginning. But soon, moved by the self-sacrificing service of the nurse, Brother Philip gave in. This further loss of control following upon his loss of mobility succeeded in breaking down the last resistance of self-defense. The loving care of fellow monks and the dedicated presence of the feminine worked together to soften his hardness of heart and, with God's grace, rendered the profound transformation in him possible.

I came to the community when Brother Philip was already

in a wheelchair. Instead of a severe and sour monk, I only knew him as a gentle, kind-hearted grandfather, always serene, calm, and wearing a smile on his face. I never heard a word of complaint from him. Let me conclude with one of his wisdom sayings: "The mills of God grind slow, but exceeding fine." By the grace of God, Brother Philip's patient endurance during the sickness of the last decade of his life turned "Philip the terrible" into the legendary loving grandpa of the Hermitage.

*Virginia Gray Henry*

Fourteen years ago, I was paralyzed with a great deal of pain for a year. At the time, I was living in England but for the winter was taken to the Middle East because it was warmer. I asked some of the women there, "How do you view illness of this magnitude?" They replied, "We consider all illness a great blessing from God, because it is intended to purify you of even the least bad things you have done." In fact, if you ask someone in that part of the world, "How are you?" even if they have something terrible wrong with them, all they will say is "Alleluia. All praise to God." They will never directly answer your question.

As I was thinking about this, I thought to myself, "Well, I suppose I've *really* been blessed." Then, all of a sudden, I realized that instead of merely tolerating the illness, I was actually loving God's will for me because he had honored me with something that big. That very moment, when I let go, stopped resisting the illness, and instead started flowing with the illness and with God's will in it, my fingers began to move.

### *Prioress Margaret Michaud*

Often when we experience serious illness, we get caught up in the health-care industry, which in my experience can be very inhumane in a lot of ways. There is a lack of care for the entire person. I remember one time one of our older sisters, who didn't quite know her own limitations, started cleaning the trunk room and got her back all out of kilter. I had to find a physician for her to see and remember the first inquiry I made, when the receptionist said, "Doctor is not taking any more backs." I thought, "Well, to them Sister is just a back." So often there is this detachment, as when you hear nurses asking one another, "How is that gallbladder in room 205?" I really believe that part of our monastic witness is to show others how to care for the entire person.

### Judith Simmer-Brown

Some of our students do hospital chaplain internships. They are trained in Buddhist *taking-and-giving* practice, which they do when they are in the hospital. This practice is incredibly powerful in working with suffering, one's own and the suffering of others. Sometimes they go into hospital rooms where people are in great suffering, even dying. They take in the suffering of the sick or dying person and give back peace and care. By doing this compassionate practice at the bedside, they contribute to a peaceful and caring atmosphere in the room. Also, by being open to the suffering, they learn with peace and care more about their own mortality.

### Lama Eric Marcoux

For me, the following story is a touching reminder that we can always make someone's life better, even if they are dying from an illness. We just have to make ourselves one with them. About fifteen years ago, I received a call from a male nurse. He said, "I have a Buddhist client who is dying, and I really need some information." We exchanged information and then he told me this story.

He said that he had been working in a hospital and a young Catholic monk was one of his patients. The young monk was dying of AIDS. Now, that was many years ago, and his monastic community was not allowed to know his circumstances. So, the young monk was dying with his family in the outer hall, but his community was not there.

The nurse said to him, "Is there anything that you've never done that you wish you could do before you die?"

"Yes," replied the young monk, "I've never danced with anyone."

"Ah," said the nurse. "My room is in this hospital. Let me get my turntable and a Frank Sinatra record."

When the nurse returned, he lifted the young monk out of the bed, put the monk's feet on top of his own feet, placed their arms around each other, and danced to Frank Sinatra. Afterward, the nurse put the monk in his bed, went out to the family, and said, "He's yours now." The young monk died within an hour.

### Ajahn Amaro

Certainly in a contemplative life, one of the skills that is so important is to be able to receive painful emotional experiences where we meet the feeling of powerlessness, the lack of control. That feeling of losing control can lead us to deny or flee from the pain.

So, it is important to resist this survival impulse and stay with the painful experience, to see it for what it really is. It is not that we want the pain but to see what is so painful. It may be an experience of rejection or failure, grief or loss, being useless or not having done anything important with our life. We need to face the truth, receive it into our hearts, and digest it. In that digestion there is an acceptance as we become one with our painful experience—just like in eating food.

In the cases of mature spiritual living, persons can move through this acceptance into the realization of what is beyond the sickness, the pain, the aging. This beyond is unborn and deathless, and in it we find ultimate freedom. In this way, aging and sickness can actually make us more serious about our spiritual life. In Buddhism it is said that one cannot find the treasure without entering the sea of suffering.

### Kate Olson

I was struck by that while Christianity and Buddhism have two different visions for understanding suffering, they end up at the same point in their practice—the practice of not clinging, of letting go. It's interesting to hear about differences between the traditions, but my ears really perk up when you touch on what they have in common. Emphasizing the common ground in practice and experience would help extend the fruits of dialogue beyond the monastery to laypeople who have a "contemplative heart."

### Father Thomas Ryan

I would like to share an experience of how I've been working with both Christian and Buddhist perspectives with regard to sickness, aging, and death in a retreat setting. When I turned fifty years old, I didn't just want to have another birthday party. I wanted to do something that had some significance. So I invited family and friends who wanted to join me in this to come to our retreat center and to spend a weekend meditating and discussing, reflecting on how we face our mortality. It turned out to be such a worthwhile experience that I have continued to do it once or twice a year.

After constant refinement and attunement, I have structured the whole retreat around the following four Buddhist assertions: I am subject to sickness; sickness is unavoidable. I am subject to aging; aging is unavoidable. I am subject to death; death is unavoidable. I will be separated from all that I hold dear; separation is unavoidable.

This forms the scaffolding for the retreat. At each point I ask people to get in touch with a personal experience of sickness, aging, or separation, and we use this as a point of departure. I'm well served in this retreat by some of the meditations on sickness, aging, and death that come from the Buddhist tradition. From the Christian perspective, it is a very rich opportunity for us to apply our conviction that every new experience of life comes only through an experience of dying or letting go. In Christian spirituality, this is called the paschal mystery, the passing over through death to new life, which is seen in its fullest expression in the resurrection.

The challenge is for us to identify how we live this letting go in a daily way in our aging process. Where are all the little places each day that I live the letting go or the dying experience, come to face my fears, and see what happens when I do that? How does doing so bring me to an experience of new life, deeper understanding, greater compassion?

I find this to be a very rich mix, this working with perspectives from the two faiths to the point where it has become a favorite retreat theme, both in ecumenical and interfaith settings, because we all have to pass through this door. We are all concerned with death. We all have fears around it. The wisdom that I see coming from each religion is that the best way to prepare for death is to anticipate it in little pieces here and now, to modulate our fears by anticipating it in small ways when we are alive.

In one sense, it is like practicing for the Big Letting Go on the installment plan. What becomes clear is that death and re-birth/resurrection are not just ultimate events but immediate sequences—our evolutionary life changes, the coming and go-ing of the seasons, good-byes and hellos—and daily choices every step of the journey. When we experience for ourselves the inner freedom that comes from learning to let go before things are taken finally from us, we see that death need not have its sting.

# CHAPTER ELEVEN

# *Facing Death*

## THE FINAL JOURNEY FROM
## FEAR TO PEACE

***Prioress Margaret Michaud***
The fear of death is very real for many people. Often in my experience people will say, "Why is this happening to me? What have I ever done to deserve this?" The whole person is affected at the time of a serious, life-threatening illness. Our society, of course, takes a very negative view of sickness and death, realities that are to be avoided at all costs. We have all sorts of remedies that are sold to us daily so that we never have to be in pain. Denial of sickness and death is part of our culture.

When we look at our Christian Scriptures, we see a whole different attitude, and this affects the outlook of persons who take these Scriptures seriously. Let me describe the death of one of our sisters a few months ago. Sister Marilyn had lung cancer, but for a long time we didn't know it. We were kind of doctoring her all last summer, for she had anemia and some pain, but we weren't quite sure what it was all about until finally it was diagnosed as lung cancer. I was with her when the doctor gave her the news. He told her very gently and appropriately that she was very ill and that there really was no treatment because the illness had progressed so far. I wasn't sure that she understood what he had said, so after he left the room, I started telling her, "Now, you know this is very serious, this news that you received." But she sat straight up in bed, looked me right in the eye, and said, "I am so glad I had some time here on planet earth!"

Sister Marilyn's response just floored me. She was an artist and a true contemplative spirit, someone who loved nature and was the kind of person who was always wandering outside, listening to the birds, watching the deer and enjoying nature. And yet she was able to look forward to her death with the greatest joy.

Of all the deaths that I've observed, this was one of the happiest, the most joyful. When Sister could no longer live in her own room, she went to our nursing facility, where we took care of her. Each day it seemed like she became more radiant. She would sometimes ask me, "Am I doing this right? What am I supposed to be doing? Am I doing it right?" All I could say was, "Well, Marilyn, I don't know. I've never been through this myself. I've seen a lot of people go through it, but I really can't tell you how to do it."

On the final evening when she died, after she had received the Eucharist and the sisters had all gathered around her, we sang and prayed and sat with her through the night. About midnight she became unresponsive, and just as the sun was coming up she left us. I think what made her death such a wonderful experience for all of us was largely her own attitude, her joyfulness. But it was also the presence of the community, those of us who were there with her, supporting her. It was an experience of grace, one of the richest blessings of monastic life.

### Father Julian von Duerbeck

Our community has a couple of practices that help us become more at peace about death. One is that on the eve of the anniversary of the death of every monk who has gone before us, his life story is read in the refectory during our evening meal. These stories include all the humorous and sorrowful things that marked their lives, their successes and even some of their failures. They are never forgotten in the community, and this is part of the unity that gives encouragement to others.

Second, on All Souls Day in early November, we all go to the abbey cemetery and hear chanted the name of every monk who is buried there. As a medieval monastic writer said about someone in the community who had died, "The memory of that person, his merry voice, his joyful countenance, his words of inspiration are always with me."

All this is part of what it means to act out of the paschal mystery. We are continually dying and rising together, and our seeing this in the lives and deaths of our confreres brings us peace about our own death.

~

### Venerable Henepola Gunaratana

From the Buddhist point of view, there are actually three kinds of deaths. First is momentary death. We are dying and taking rebirth every moment. Meditators are advised to contemplate this momentary death as a means of preparing our mind to face death peacefully.

The second type is conventional death, when one actually dies. People try to avoid thinking of this kind of death, but we try to prepare ourselves by contemplating our future death. Why? Because everyone experiences confusion and fear when facing death. It is natural. It is important to find peace at the time of death, and our practice helps us find that peace when the time comes. We believe that this last moment is extremely important. We call death "proximate karma," the karmic state of the person that strongly affects his or her next life.

We try to help those who are dying to find this peace so that they will be reborn in a peaceful, happy place. Sometimes we go into the dying person's home, stand by his or her bed, and recite certain *sutras* to console the person, to make the person feel comfortable and peaceful. Also, we deliver a sermon explaining the meaning of life and death, and we remind the dying person about all the good things he or she has done.

The third kind of death is the pure death of Parinirvana, final Nirvana. When one's mind is completely free from all psychic irritants and defilements, when one's mind is totally free and pure, one passes to final Nirvana. It is believed that such a person can also come back from the moment of pure death in order to relieve the pain of others, just as the Buddha did. When the Buddha attained this pure death, he did so in the highest state of meditation. At that moment his closest disciple, Ananda, who had not attained that state of enlightenment, began to cry. In a compassionate response, the Buddha came back from his highest state of meditation and relieved the mind of Ananda. This happened with the Buddha and also with other enlightened persons.

### Geshe Lhundub Sopa

Religions present two approaches to death. One is the way of faith and the other is the way of realization. Most people follow the way of faith both in Buddhism and Christianity. In both religions there is faith in the power of a savior to bring one to a better life after death. In Buddhism we have many celestial Buddhas and bodhisattvas into whose care people entrust themselves with faith. It is like these divine powers have a hook to lift people up after death. But people need a ring for the hook to catch. Faith provides that ring. This understanding of death is very helpful in developing a peaceful attitude toward it.

### Venerable Guo Yuan Fa Shi

In our Buddhist organization, we practice what we call "compassion for the dying" in order to strengthen people's faith. When a member of our organization is about to pass away, a group of our people goes to the hospital or the home to recite the name of the Amitabha Buddha, the Buddha of the Pure Land, where many Buddhists want to be born after death. This helps not only the person who is passing away but also the family members. Through this chanting practice, we try to enable the dying person to let go, or put down, his or her attachments to this world. This is the most important thing, helping the dying find peace and acceptance. When the family sees the dying person at peace, they too find a deeper acceptance of the passing of a loved one.

### Father Joseph Wong

I find the Jesus Prayer, the constant invocation of the name of Jesus, very similar to the invocation of the name of Buddha as it is practiced in Pure Land Buddhism. The Jesus Prayer started with the desert fathers, then spread to Mount Sinai, and from there to Greece and Eastern Europe, including Russia. Since the middle of the last century, it has also become very much diffused in the Western church. Nowadays many Christians are committed to this path of the Jesus Prayer. Its traditional formula is: "Lord Jesus Christ, Son of God, have mercy on me." Even this phrase can be shortened to, for example, "Lord Jesus, have mercy!"

Just as many Buddhists invoke the Amitabha Buddha at the bedside of someone who is dying, we have the practice of reciting the Jesus Prayer in the presence of a dying person. For example, several years ago in our community an elderly brother was dying. He had been sick for some time, and when he was near death most of the brothers in our community would spend time at his bedside. During the last couple of days, I tried to help him by reciting the Jesus Prayer. This brought him much comfort in the midst of suffering. Sometimes I recited the Our Father or the Hail Mary, but most of the time I was reciting the Jesus Prayer, sitting just next to him so that he could hear. I could see that he felt so peaceful, so serene when hearing the repetition of the name of Jesus and the invocation of his mercy. I think this is probably the best way to accompany a fellow Christian during the last hour of his or her passage from this life, for it allows one to make the passage in the company of Jesus and his mercy.

### Father Mark Delery

As a physician who has been in practice for more than fifty years, I've seen many people die. I'd just like to mention two illustrative cases.

At one of our abbeys there was a nice, old Irishman who had been born and raised Catholic and had spent his life in the monastery as a cheerful, simple monk. As he was dying from cancer of the stomach, one of the younger monks, a very fervent convert, visited him in his sickroom while I was in attendance. The young monk said, "Oh, Brother, we want you to know we appreciate your suffering. You are truly a victim soul." He went on in this vein for a while, and when he departed the old monk turned to me and said, "I wish he would cut out all that pious crap."

My second illustration concerns my sister, a rosary-reciting Catholic who died recently of colon cancer in a city close to my monastery. So I was able to visit her a number of times, finding her always uncomplaining. When she was approaching the end of her life in a hospice room, I asked her: "Do you have any questions?" She replied, "No. I didn't think it was going to be this easy."

### Father William Skudlarek

After about five years living in Japan, it became more and more clear to me that Japan was not the place where I would be able to spend the rest of my life, for a lot of different reasons. Then when I was back home at my abbey in Minnesota, I went to speak with our new abbot, just to see how things were and without any expectation of an early return to the States. But he asked me if I would come back in that very year to be his assistant.

That came as wonderful news, totally unexpected news. I went back to Japan to wrap things up there, and every morning when I got up, the first thought in my mind was: "I'm going home. I'm going home."

Sometime later, while preparing to give a retreat, I dealt with Benedict's injunction to keep death daily before one's eyes. Suddenly that's what his phrase meant to me: "I'm going home." If one looks at death in that way, it's not some depressing thought about one's life coming to an end. No, it means I'm going home. This suddenly reshaped the whole way I think about my death.

## Abbot John Daido Loori

We spent about two weeks with a *Sangha* member, who was slowly dying an agonizing death. A lot of our monks came to be with him, to hold his hand, to talk and listen, and to chant. Coming into this kind of direct contact with a very painful death throws all the theory about death and dying out the window. It reaches really deep inside and does something to us that all of the textbooks, lectures, and even sitting meditation do not do. The direct experience of someone suffering and dying transforms everybody around him or her in a very special way. How, I don't know; but I do know that it happens. I've seen it.

I would also like to share about when my mother was at the end of her life. She was in her late eighties in Florida and had really severe Alzheimer's. She didn't recognize any of the family. My brother called me to say that she was nearing the end, so I went to Florida and I sat with her.

She had no idea who I was. I had brought her a rose, and that triggered something. She just sat there rocking and muttering, "Rose, Rose, where is Rose?" I wanted so desperately to help her. It was clear from the look on her face that she was frightened. She knew the end was near, and she was scared to death.

So, here I am, a Buddhist priest sitting with my Catholic mother. I have dedicated my whole life to helping people. I do it all the time. But I didn't have the tools to reach her, to help her. Then suddenly I thought, "What has been the continuing center of Mother's life going all the way back to when she was a little girl?" It was prayer. So I said to her, "Do you want to pray? Would you like to pray with me?"

When I said "pray," she looked at me. I'll never forget her look. Her eyes just penetrated mine, and she didn't say yes or no. So I started praying the Hail Mary and the Our Father. Her lips started moving. She was kind of saying the prayers quietly to herself. And then I switched to Italian, which was her original language, and her voice then came into it. She closed her eyes and I watched her face transform—so quiet, so angelic—and she fell asleep in the chair.

The nurse came and I helped her put my mother in the bed. The next morning when I came to see her at the nursing home, the nurse said that she had never woken up from that sleep. In helping a person find peace at the moment of death, the method is not so important, it's the heart behind it that makes the difference.

### Samu Sunim

No one is saved from suffering except through suffering—through suffering for others. Examples of what I mean can be seen in the lives of traditional Korean Son (Zen) Buddhist teachers when facing death. Some of them endure great suffering at death. But even then, they endure it for the sake of others. They maintain awakened consciousness while they die sitting up. That is the tradition.

How is this a sign of compassion? Their manner of dying is witnessed by the many disciples surrounding them. By dying in that way, their suffering and death is an encouragement in the spiritual life that the disciples will never forget. Also, by dying in this way, the masters will carry their enlightened consciousness through to the next life. They will be reborn such that the candle of their enlightened consciousness will light the candle of their next life with that awakened awareness. So they will come back to the world in order to help others over-come suffering and attain liberation. In this way, their form of death is an act of compassion in itself.

### *Abbot John Daido Loori*

Master Tozan, seeing that his end was near, shaved his head, bathed himself, put on his robes, and sat cross-legged, prepar-ing to die. As he began to expire, his very large congregation started wailing and carrying on . . . the wailing went on and on and on.

Finally Tozan opened his eyes and said, "For those who have left home, a mind unattached to things is the true prac-tice. People struggle to live and make much of death. What's the use of lamenting?"

Then Tozan ordered a temple official to prepare for what he called "a banquet for stupidity." Everybody celebrated, and Tozan himself joined in the celebration. But the community's concern about his health did not stop, so Tozan continued the celebration for seven days. Finally Tozan said, "You monks have made a great commotion over nothing. When you see me pass away this time, don't make a noisy fuss." Then he retired to his room, sat upright, and left his body.

Now, lest you think that this is something that happens only with great Zen masters, my grandmother, who was a peas-ant from the mountains of Italy and was in her late eighties, was ill and lying in bed. My mother was with her. Eventually my grandmother expired. As her lips and fingers started turning blue, my mother started wailing. She was a very passionate Italian daughter. And my grandmother sucked in air again and sat upright. Then my mother calmed her down again, she lay back, and again she expired. Again my mother started wailing, and again my grandmother returned. Her daughter was crying out to her, so she couldn't go.

Finally my mother realized what she was doing. She was preventing her mother from leaving her body. So she told her mother, "It's okay, Mom. It's okay to let go." And she finally did expire.

I think my grandmother's return for her daughter's sake shows us the great heart of compassion that resides in every one of us. If we look, look at the great religious teachers, the great saints, the great religious founders like Jesus and Buddha, we see the realization and living out of this great heart of compassion. Now it is in our hands to realize this reality that is deep within us and live it for the benefit of everyone. It may seem a hopeless task, yet we vow to do it.

I think that we can turn and bow to our spiritual ancestors, and take up their dedication to the compassionate healing of the world. Then we can transform our suffering, even our dying, as did Tozan and my grandmother, in order to administer compassionate healing to others.

### Father James Wiseman

It is very important to strengthen a person's faith at the time of death. Our teachings about an afterlife do that. But if we are to avoid presenting Christian doctrine as something just totally absurd, it's very important to recognize that when we speak of what comes beyond death, we would do well to use a medieval distinction that some of the best theologians today also make, the distinction between knowing and believing. We believe that a good person will live eternally with God, but we don't know exactly what comes on the other side of death. When I speak of my Christian hope of living forever with Christ, body and soul, it is totally impossible to imagine just what that will be like. To be with God forever, "body and soul," means that your whole person will be fully in the divine presence. It's pointless to try to go into greater detail than that.

### Father Damon Geiger

The resurrection of the dead is not the resuscitation of a corpse but the entrance into a fullness of life that has no death. We don't know just what this fullness is because from the moment we are born, we are a mixture of life and death. The older we get, every time we look in the mirror we see that there is less hair, more wrinkles, and things like that. We simply don't know a state of pure life. The resurrection, however, means that we will be raised to a state where there is no longer this mixture of death and life.

In all the churches of Roman Catholicism and Eastern Orthodoxy, a great feast is celebrated on or around August 15. It is often called the *Dormition,* that is, the falling asleep of Mary, the Mother of God. This feast actually celebrates what death is for us as Christians. Its iconography shows Mary, the archetypical Christian, falling asleep in death. The same meaning crops up in our word "cemetery," which literally means a sleeping chamber. A cemetery is not a place for dead people. It's a place where people are sleeping.

### Donald Mitchell

One distinction that has helped me understand a bit more about the meaning of the resurrection of the body is the New Testament distinction between *sarx* and *soma. Sarx* is "flesh" and is not what resurrects. If so, we would have the resurrection of a corpse. *Soma* refers to the whole embodied person. In the Jewish tradition, this embodied personhood is very important because our body in this sense is what enables us to have personal relationships. So what resurrects, then, is our whole embodied personhood, which enables us to relate to one another and to God forever.

### Father Joseph Wong

While agreeing that the resurrection is the most important meaning of the statement that "Christ has conquered death," I would like to reflect on another implication of that statement: that is, that Christ has given a new meaning to death. Due to the finite existence of humans, death itself is a natural phenomenon, eliciting anxiety, uncertainty, and suffering. In accepting a most painful death, Christ has given a new redemptive meaning to death by turning what was seen as a sign of punishment from God into a supreme expression of loving obedience and total surrender to the Father.

The fact that Christ has given a new meaning to death has opened up the possibility for us to participate in, or appropriate, his salvific death. In this regard, Karl Rahner, the well-known German theologian, has offered a profound reflection on the meaning of death. On one hand, death is seen as something most passive, which humans simply undergo without much to say about its time or place. On the other hand, however, death is something potentially most active, a personal event.

As death is something that takes place once only, it can be seen as the most important moment of one's life, a time when one is summoned to make a final decision regarding oneself. In the face of death, one can either adopt an attitude of rebellious refusal, thus repeating the disobedience of Adam, or else appropriate Christ's loving acceptance and obedience to the Father. If we look at our life as a long love letter addressed to God, the personal decision made at the hour of death can be compared to our signature, which confirms our lifelong dedication to God.

☙

## Father Thomas Keating

One of the problems of the spiritual journey is dis-identifying ourselves with our ideas of our self or over-identifying ourselves with our feelings, bodies, roles, or groups. As Jesus stated, "Unless you renounce your inmost self, you can't be my disciples." So, any self-identity is itself an obstacle to the fullness of the Christian life, if we are stuck on it.

The Christian life, it seems to me, does not end with Christ's resurrection. This is a major step, but when we say we follow Christ, it's not just down the roads of Galilee, or to Jerusalem, or to Calvary, or even to the resurrection. It is a journey to the ascension, which is Christ's return to the bosom of the Father.

It's in this mystery that Buddhists and Christians have the greatest chance of meeting, because it is in that place that there is no self as we know it, no fixed point of reference. Instead, there is an openness to the Ultimate Reality in which there is only the identity of the Absolute Self and our relation to it.

### Venerable Guo Yuan Fa Shi

Is there life after death? Many Buddhists have this belief, especially the Pure Land practitioners. They believe in the compassionate vow of Amitabha Buddha, who could help them attain the heavenly Pure Land after death. There they will advance in the spiritual life as a bodhisattva and eventually come back to this cycle of birth and death in order to help sentient beings. This is one important Buddhist notion of life after death.

In Ch'an (Zen) practice, the emphasis is not to rely on Amitabha Buddha, but on yourself. When you reach liberation, you are free to come and go into this cycle of birth and death. In this Ch'an tradition, there is an ancient story about Bodhidharma, the monk who legend says brought the Ch'an tradition to China from India. The story says that when Bodhidharma passed away, he was put in a coffin and buried. Later the coffin was unearthed, and in it they could only find one sandal, just one sandal. The tradition says that many people remembered seeing a lone monk traveling toward India wearing only one sandal.

What this story illustrates is that in his liberated state, Bodhidharma is free to come and go at will. For him, life after death is not an issue.

❧

### Ajahn Amaro

In the story of the Buddha's enlightenment, the Buddha is depicted as being assailed by Mara, a spirit who tempts people to get them to remain in this world of birth and death. Mara's realm is where there is death. So enlightenment is actually depicted as the conquest of death. In Theravada, we talk about the realization of the "deathless." It is common to refer to the initial experience of enlightenment as the realization of the deathless, of that dimension which is unborn, undying, timeless, intrinsically transcendent. We are speaking here of Nirvana. It is in the realization of Nirvana that we can conquer death as did the Buddha.

### Joseph Goldstein

In Christianity, God is experienced as Ultimate Reality. In Theravada Buddhism, the experience of the Ultimate is what we would call Nirvana, and one's first dip into Nirvana is called entering the stream. This experience of Nirvana has the power to cut off karma, which would lead to rebirth into realms of suffering. So, immersion in the stream uproots, or takes away, the effects of our unwholesome actions in a way that may be similar to how immersion in God heals and frees one from sin and death. I think the difference would be that some Buddhist traditions would see this healing and freeing as a function of the purity of the absolute, without personalizing it.

I would add that one Buddhist view of death is that it can be looked at in two ways. There is an ultimate dimension that is not born and does not die, and a relative dimension that lives and dies. There are waves that come and go, and there is water that never changes.

This is illustrated in a story about the death of His Holiness the Sixteenth Karmapa Lama. He died near Chicago from cancer. At his deathbed, his disciples were grieving, and at one point he turned to them and said, "Don't worry. Nothing happens."

### Abbot John Daido Loori

Being free of life and death is found when we realize life as unborn and death as unextinguished. In birth, nothing arrives; and in death, nothing leaves. What this is alluding to is the fact that ordinarily I think that everything inside my bag of skin is me and everything outside is the rest of the universe. What must be realized is that this very body and mind is the body and mind of the universe. When that primordial fact is realized, then we can say: "In birth, nothing is added. In death, nothing is lost." This for Zen is like conquering death.

### *Zenkei Blanche Hartman*

There is a story about a Zen master:

A student asks: "What happens when you die?"

The master replies, "I don't know."

The student responds, "What do you mean you don't know? Aren't you a Zen master?"

The master answers, "Yes, but I'm not a dead one!"

# CHAPTER TWELVE

# *Building a Culture of Dialogue and Peace*

***His Holiness the Dalai Lama***
I believe that meetings between members of different spiritual traditions, exploring and sharing each other's experiences, have the potential to make a real practical contribution to a greater peace and understanding in our world. Everyone already knows my personal enthusiasm for this work, and I pray for the fruitful success of this dialogue.

### Father Damien Thompson

All of us in this troubled era need to stretch ourselves to attain the peace and unity the world is seeking. To do this, we need a listening heart to enable ourselves to reach over the walls that societies have always used to exclude others for the sake of their own identity. This image of a listening heart is one that society needs today. We need people of dialogue who are capable of stretching themselves beyond their own parameters, who realize there is something important in life beyond their boundaries. The *Rule* of Benedict states very early on that we have to hear with the ears of the heart. If we truly listen with our hearts, we discover that we are all brothers and sisters in the truest sense of the word. What separates us today, tomorrow will be a memory. We belong to one human family.

During the Gethsemani Encounter in 1996, when the Dalai Lama was present, there was an incident that happened in a very private moment that was so expressive of a listening heart. It happened in one of those casual moments when everyone was in a crush, passing from the church into the monastery chapter room for one of the discussions. Everyone was distracted by those who happened to be bumping against them. But the Dalai Lama, with great respect and with no intention of impressing anyone, just happened to pass in front of the Blessed Sacrament, which is central to our faith. And he paused in the privacy of his own moment to bow respectfully to the Blessed Sacrament, and then he moved on. There was no intention at the time of impressing anyone, but he happened to be seen, and his gesture deepened the faith of one who saw this.

*Zoketsu Norman Fischer*

Friendship is a tremendously powerful source of healing. When friends share about their suffering, hearts fall open, persons connect, and communion happens. A listening heart, a caring heart soothes our anxieties. We are no longer alone, and we can be honest about our deepest fears and confusions. We can share our inadequacies and our wounds as well as our aspirations and dreams.

When good, sincere, wise, and kind people of different faiths are friends, when they meet and support each other in deep interfaith sharing, powerful things can happen. Wonderful changes can happen. The whole world benefits. By being together in solidarity, compassion, and peacefulness, with all our differences, we are a living solution to many of the world's troubles. We are a living sign of what the world needs.

So, how do we offer our practices dedicated to goodness, peace, and love—with their different flavors—to the world that is facing troubling times today? I think that the virtue of interfaith dialogue is that the more we dialogue together, the more we come to some unity in living our religious lives while also recognizing the real differences in flavor. This can be a sign to the world that it is possible to have a more united humankind if people make the choice to seek goodness, wholeness, and peace.

Monastic communities, Buddhist and Christian, are repositories of sanity, peace, love, and wisdom. Our world needs these spiritual treasures now more than ever. The mystery of Jesus' death and resurrection, and the meaning and power of Buddha's enlightenment, are not merely historical events. They are the means of great healing for ourselves and the world. They are especially present in the heart of interfaith friendship as a spirit of openness and wonder, love and compassion, healing and freedom.

I once thought that interfaith dialogue was a polite and harmless little thing, mildly amusing if you had the time for it. But now I see it as powerfully transformative because interfaith spiritual friendship is a healing light for our world. In that light, we can see each other with new eyes and discover ourselves anew. So, the real challenge and gift of interfaith dialogue is to be willing to listen and have your own religious position utterly questioned within yourself. It is not that you lose your faith but that when you have confidence enough to let go of how you understand your tradition's teachings and really listen to the other person, your own tradition comes alive in a deeper way.

For example, I have come to appreciate the strength and beauty of the Christian community and of the Christian message. I have seen through my Christian brothers and sisters why Jesus really matters so much. Christians are taught to see a suffering person as Jesus himself. This is a powerful thought: The suffering person, the unfortunate person, the despised person is God, is the Absolute. Now I too can see Jesus as the power and mystery of transformative suffering in this world. So, I am strengthened in my conviction that suffering is not just something to get rid of but to embrace and understand. This insight has made a real difference in my life. I am a better Buddhist, with greater courage, energy, and compassion to go ahead in my Buddhist journey.

Having said all this, I have to make a confession. When I first saw how beautiful Christianity is, and how I could really take it into my heart in my own way, it was a disturbing thing. I had to reckon with all the wounding that a Jew feels in relation to Christianity. I grew up among Catholic friends but never really discussed their religion. I actually felt, I'm sorry to say, that Catholicism was a mild form of insanity, a mild form of insanity that might end up being harmful to my health; so I'd better be careful.

When I first began to realize the beauty of Jesus and all its many dimensions that you find in the Catholic tradition, I found it extremely mysterious, disturbing, powerful, and really sad. I have experienced this in the Mass. The Mass has really affected me, and this is disturbing to me as a Jew. But somehow it didn't take too long to work through that disturbance to see what would happen next. What happened was that I went back to the study of Hebrew Bible and Jewish meditation practice. My oldest friend is a rabbi, and now we are practicing together.

🌿

### Father Leo Lefebure

The Buddhist tradition teaches us that we are intimately interconnected. There is no North or South, no East or West in the Buddha-nature. This insight into unity is not a monopoly of Buddhists. The Letter to the Colossians tells us that all things hold together in Christ and that Christ has reconciled all things in heaven and on earth. This is not a monopoly of Christians. We can realize the truth of these teachings in the twofold sense of becoming conscious of them in a new way and of making real the connections among us. Think of the impact that the friendship between Thomas Merton and His Holiness the Dalai Lama has had on Buddhists and Christians around the world. If properly nurtured and fostered, the unity between people of different faiths can help shape the broader global community that our world so desperately needs.

Interfaith encounter is an opportunity for profound spiritual renewal as well as challenge and change. In this context, the encounter with Buddhists has often come as a breath of fresh air for Christians. The challenge of Theravadin teachers of meditation, "Acknowledge, acknowledge, acknowledge," resonates deeply with the age-old Christian spiritual quest. The insistence of Ch'an and Son teachers to experience reality oneself directly and not simply to parrot the teachings of others reinforces Bernard of Clairvaux's goal of believing in order to experience for oneself. The practices, the poetry, the art, the calligraphy, the rock gardens, the narratives of Buddhism come as gifts that enable Christians to look at matters from a different perspective, providing fresh insights into one's own heritage.

For example, we Christians have the teaching about God as totally other than this world, as the creator, the giver of the act of existence. But there is a whole strand of the Christian tradition, represented by people like Bonaventure, Meister Eckhart, and Nicholas of Cusa, that emphasizes that we exist in the mind of God. In the mind of God, as he created us, we are all united. From this perspective, my existence in the mind of God is my most real existence, for the way God knows me is more true than my own imperfect knowledge of myself. Looked at in this way, in a real sense we are all one, and yet there is *also* the reality of creation itself with all its diversity.

We know that throughout its history, Buddhism has been very bold, creative, and innovative in coming into new cultures; and today there is a new inculturation of Buddhism in Western culture. We welcome the presence of venerable Asian teachers, many of whom have lived in this country for years and have become familiar with American culture and customs. There is also an increasingly mature Euro-American practice of Buddhism, which gives a fresh voice to ancient Buddhist teachings and practices. We encounter Euro-American Buddhists steeped in the wisdom of the Buddhist tradition while coming from a culture long shaped by Judaism and Christianity. Often there is a willingness to look at traditional Buddhist teachings in a new light in relation to Judaism and Christianity, an openness to experimenting with terminology, and an openness to making comparisons across traditions.

Often Euro-American Buddhists bring a distinct relation to Judaism or Christianity, which can shape both their practice of Buddhism and also their relation to Jews and Christians today. What happens when a Jew or a Christian becomes a Buddhist? A few years ago Robert Aitken Roshi told me that he is still a Christian, and he has written publicly about this. He told me that he was so bored in the Christian churches of his youth that he thought he would not remember anything. But decades later, when he guides his students in Zen practice, the stories and sayings of Jesus and other biblical figures rise up in his mind and shape his leadership. He noted in particular the impact of the concern for social justice in the Christian tradition upon his own development of engaged Buddhist practice.

In my own case, the practice of mindfulness has had a great effect on me. When I first entered a Theravada Buddhist monastery in the north of Thailand in 1986, I was in no way ready for it. The monastic teacher there wanted me to meditate twenty-four hours a day! Talk about an impossible situation, especially in the evening when the salamanders would be all over the walls, walking back and forth. It was almost impossible to keep my mindfulness.

Some years later I made a *vipassana* (insight meditation) retreat, and all kinds of things came up. It was very healthy, very healing, very cleansing for me. After wrestling with a number of different issues, one day I was just walking in the afternoon in my room, doing walking meditation back and forth, when completely out of the blue came an overwhelming sense that everything would be okay in my life. It wasn't that things would go well outwardly but that even in the face of the worst possible catastrophes in my life, I wouldn't have to worry. Many times on Catholic retreats I had prayed "Thy will be done," but on this *vipassana* retreat things moved to a whole other level. I myself was out of the way. It was a very moving experience. Being more aware of myself, being more present, being more stable, being better able to handle difficulties—all this has been a wonderful gift from Buddhism.

### Father Felix Machado

The Catholic Church has made an irreversible commitment to interreligious dialogue. We see this in the documents of Vatican II and in the words of the popes and Vatican statements ever since. We say that all people have a role in this dialogue. We all need to become people of dialogue in working for world peace.

The first kind of dialogue is the dialogue of life, of sharing our faith with others and learning from others about their faith as well. My father was a gardener in India living with people of other religions. Dialogue in the most positive sense ensured peace with one's neighbors, recognizing what is true, noble, and laudable in the other persons' religions. This village model is one for the whole world.

There is also the dialogue of collaboration, working together for a better, more just and peaceful world. The dialogue of theological discussion helps clarify teachings, practices, and values, contributing to better mutual understanding and respect between peoples. The dialogue of religious experience shares about the depths of our traditions' spiritualities, bringing us to a deeper spiritual unity.

On the other hand, some people think interreligious dialogue is like an ambulance that you call when there is some conflict or violence. I particularly have in mind the violence in India between Hindus and Muslims and between Hindus and Christians. For example, in 1992, soon after Hindus demolished the mosque at Ayodhya, in Bombay alone a chain of sixteen bombs went off in the span of one hour. Among those killed was a cousin of mine.

I was in Bombay at that time, and very involved in interreligious dialogue with very good friends across the spectrum of the various religions. At the time of the bombings, I received phone calls from people all asking "Where is your interreligious dialogue now? Why doesn't it work? Why are you wasting your time with that?" These people thought that interreligious dialogue is a solution that we should be able to apply at the eleventh hour. But it doesn't work that way.

Therefore, I very much agree with what His Holiness the Dalai Lama has said: Hatred is the root cause of violence. So if we want peace, we need to address religious misunderstanding and prejudice by building a culture of dialogue, as Pope John Paul II suggests. Otherwise, we will continue the present clash of cultures, with all its violence, seen most clearly on September 11. Today our spiritual traditions have much to say to us about our common humanity, much to contribute to peace and understanding. We are fellow pilgrims in this world, and we need to recognize our unity within our diversity and work together to build a more united and peaceful world for the sake of all humankind.

# *Epilogue*

There is a tragic irony in the fact that just prior to the first Gethsemani Encounter, seven Trappist monks were killed by terrorists in North Africa, and that just after the second Gethsemani Encounter, a lone gunman killed two Benedictine monks at Conception Abbey in Missouri. We have asked Father Donald Grabner, who was at the second Gethsemani Encounter, to share his experience as a monk of Conception Abbey.

*On June 10, not quite two months after Gethsemani Encounter II that dealt with suffering and transformation, my monastery, Conception Abbey, located in a fairly remote corner of northwest Missouri, became a victim of the terrible and senseless violence that was one of the major topics of the encounter.*

*A lone gunman, for reasons still unknown, entered the first-floor hallway of our monastery, shot to death two of our monks, seriously injured two others, and then shot himself to death in our abbey church. Until noon that next day, we monks were not permitted to enter either the first floor of our monastery or our church because both were cordoned off by yellow tape labeling these areas as "crime scenes."*

*While the sudden death of two of our members was mourned by our community, we were sure they were well prepared to face this unexpected final moment of life on this earth. So, for us, their death was more of a sudden call to suffering that the community itself and its living members had to undergo. There is, of course, genuine sorrow over the loss of two confrères; there was also our great care and concern for the physical suffering Father Kenneth and Father Norbert have had to face in recuperating from their serious wounds.*

*But, if I am not mistaken, the most challenging suffering has been that of the whole community itself having to face the violation of its very home and place of worship. This violation strikes deep at the community's heart and its image of itself as a faith community witnessing to the quiet and peace of the Benedictine tradition. This feeling was only aggravated by the fact that we can discover no reason why Mr. Lloyd Jeffress should do such a terrible deed.*

*And yet, in the events following upon that June 10 date, our community is beginning to recognize, I think, that this is a kind of redemptive suffering. By it we, as followers of Christ in his passover from death to life, have been able to witness to one another and to those many, many people who have been involved in these events. Our prayers and forgiveness for Mr. Jeffress and our prayers for his family have been a testament to the values of the Gospel.*

*Our community has also been strengthened and reunited in its most basic concerns by what it has been through. And the response of those who came in multiple ways to care for us during the hours and the days and the weeks that followed those gunshots in our home and church has been astounding. We can only be humbled by the outpouring of concern and sympathy and help that has come to us from so many directions. It is certainly an echo of what we saw in New York City after September 11.*

*We are beginning, I think, to realize that the blessings coming to us from what has happened will surely outweigh the losses, as real as they may be. The notion that God often works in mysterious ways to bring about His will among us—even out of great suffering and loss—is no longer just an empty phrase but a true expression of our experience of the paschal mystery in our day-to-day life. In some way, we are all the better for it, closer to our God who loves us and shows that love in the very midst of suffering.*

# List of Contributors

**ROBERT AITKEN ROSHI** is a retired master of the Honolulu Diamond Sangha, a Zen Buddhist Society, who is now living on the Big Island of Hawai'i with his son, Tom, and his cat, Alexander. He is author of *Taking the Path of Zen, Original Dwelling Place,* and other books on Zen Buddhism.

**AJAHN AMARO** went to London University, where he earned a joint honors degree in psychology and physiology. He was ordained as a monk in the forest meditation lineage of Venerable Ajahn Cha in northeast Thailand in 1979. He trained in England from 1979 to 1995 under Venerable Ajahn Sumedho. In June 1996 Abhayagiri Forest Monastery was opened in Redwood Valley, California, where he was the founding abbot. He has taken part in numerous Buddhist and interfaith events, and has written and edited several books, including *Food for the Heart.*

**FATHER THOMAS A. BAIMA** is a priest of the Archdiocese of Chicago and provost of the University of Saint Mary of the Lake/Mundelein Seminary.

**VENERABLE THUBTEN CHODRON** is an American Buddhist nun in the Tibetan tradition. A student of His Holiness the Dalai Lama, she became a nun in 1977. She has been resident teacher at Amitabha Buddhist Centre in Singapore and at Dharma Friendship Foundation in Seattle. She has been active in interfaith dialogue for many years, especially in Jewish-Buddhist dialogue. She teaches worldwide and is the author of several books, including *Open Heart, Clear Mind; Buddhism for Beginners; Taming the Monkey Mind;* and *Working with Anger.*

**SISTER MARY COLLINS, O.S.B.,** is prioress of the Benedictine Sisters of Mount St. Scholastica in Atchison, Kansas. She is also professor emerita of the School of Religious Studies at The Catholic University of America. Her academic specializations have been liturgy, sacramental theology and ecclesiology, and religion and culture; and in that context she has received the Berakah Award from the North American Academy of Liturgy and the Michael Mathis Award from the Notre Dame Center for Pastoral Liturgy. She has also published articles on monastic themes in *Benedictines* and the *American Benedictine Review.*

**EWERT H. COUSINS,** professor emeritus, Fordham University, is the general editor of the twenty-five-volume series

*World Spirituality: An Encyclopedic History of the Religious Quest.* He is on the Monastic Interreligious Dialogue board, co-convenor of the Commission on World Spirituality, and was consultant to the Pontifical Council for Interreligious Dialogue, 1973 to 1984. He is also author of *Christ of the 21st Century* and *Bonaventure and the Coincidence of Opposites.*

**JANET KVAMME COUSINS** received her doctorate in theology from Fordham University and is a specialist in medieval Christian theology. She is an editor, researcher, bibliographer, religious educator, and author of *The Fontalis Plenitudo in the Trintiarian Theology of Bonaventure.*

**FATHER MARK DELERY, O.C.S.O.,** is a Cistercian monk of Holy Cross Abbey, Berryville, Virginia. He has been involved in Zen Buddhist retreats and the reception of Tibetan Buddhist visitors for thirty years.

**ZOKETSU NORMAN FISCHER** served as abbot of the San Francisco Zen Center from 1995 to 2000. A Zen priest and poet, he continues to serve the Zen Center as a senior Dharma teacher and is the founder and spiritual director of the Everyday Zen Foundation. He has published widely, and his latest book is *Opening to You: Zen-Inspired Translations of the Psalms.*

**SISTER MARY MARGARET FUNK, O.S.B.,** has been a member of Our Lady of Grace Monastery in Beech Grove, Indiana, since 1961. She has a graduate degree from The Catholic University of America and certification in formative spirituality. She was prioress from 1985 to 1993, and in 1994 became executive director of Monastic Interreligious Dialogue. In that capacity she coordinated the Gethsemani Encounters in 1996 and 2002 and the Benedict's Dharma Conference in 2001. She traveled to Buddhist sites in India and Tibet on MID's sixth Spiritual Exchange Program in 1995. She has published *Thoughts Matter* and *Tools Matter,* and was a contributor to *Benedict's Dharma* and *Purity of Heart.*

**PAUL GAILEY** is vice president for programs of the Fetzer Institute, where he helps to elucidate a scientific framework that better reflects the whole of human experience. He has worked at the interface among physics, biology, medicine, and mathematics and has held research and research management posts at the U.S. Environmental Protection Agency, Oak Ridge National Laboratory, and Ohio University, where he also served as associate professor of physics and astronomy.

**FATHER DAMON GEIGER, O.SS.T.**, is novice master for the American Province of the Order of the Most Holy Trinity. He has also served as pastor, retreat director, and seminary rector in the Eastern Catholic Church and has spent several years working in spiritual formation with Eastern Christians in India.

**JOSEPH GOLDSTEIN** has been leading insight and loving-kindness meditation retreats worldwide since 1974. He studied and practiced different forms of Buddhist meditation under eminent teachers from India, Burma, and Tibet. He is a cofounder of the Insight Meditation Society in Barre, Massachusetts, where he is one of the resident guiding teachers. He is currently developing The Forest Refuge, a new center in Barre for long-term meditation practice. He is the author of *One Dharma: The Emerging Western Buddhism, Insight Meditation: The Practice of Freedom, The Experience of Insight,* and coauthor of *Seeking the Heart of Wisdom* and *Insight Meditation: A Correspondence Course.*

**FATHER DONALD GRABNER, O.S.B.,** has been a Benedictine monk of Conception Abbey, Conception, Missouri, since his first monastic profession in 1949. After completing theological studies at the Collegio Sant'Anselmo, Rome, in 1957, he has held administrative positions in his monastery and taught theology and religion in the seminary conducted by Conception Abbey. Since 1980 he has been associated with Monastic Interreligious Dialogue and since 1999 has been a member of its board. In 1986 he was one of the six American monastics who were first to be hosted by Tibetan monasteries in India at the invitation of His Holiness the Dalai Lama.

**VENERABLE HENEPOLA GUNARATANA** was born in a small village in Sri Lanka and ordained at the age of twelve. He was later a teacher in India and Malaysia. He came to the United States in 1968 and has been president of the Buddhist Vihara Society of Washington, D.C. He has taught Buddhism at The American University, Georgetown University, Bucknell University, and the University of Maryland. He is now president of the Bhavana Society in West Virginia, where he teaches meditation and conducts meditation retreats. He is author of *The Path of Serenity and Insight: An Explanation of the Buddhist Jhanas* and *Mindfulness in Plain English*.

**VENERABLE GUO YUAN FA SHI** is a monk in the Dharma Drum Mountain Buddhist Association. Inspired by the teachings of Ch'an Master Sheng-yen while attending a seven-day meditation retreat in New York in 1985, Venerable Guo Yuan came to New York to study under the master. Under the discipline and guidance of Master Sheng-yen, he became fully involved in Buddhist studies and meditation. He traveled to Thailand to further his studies in 1991. He is now the abbot of the Chan Meditation Center and Dharma Drum Retreat Center in New York.

**TENZIN GYATSO, HIS HOLINESS THE FOURTEENTH DALAI LAMA,** is the spiritual leader of the Tibetan people and is considered by them to be a manifestation of the Bodhisattva Avalokitesvara. He lives in Dharamsala, India, where he leads the Tibetan Government-in-exile. In 1989 he was awarded the Nobel Peace Prize. Among his many books are *My Land and My People; Freedom in Exile; The Good Heart: A Buddhist Perspective on the Teachings of Jesus; An Open Heart; The Art of Happiness;* and *Ethics for a New Millennium.*

**ZENKEI BLANCHE HARTMAN** is currently abbess of San Francisco Zen Center. She began practicing at the Berkeley Zendo in 1969 and trained under Shunryu Suzuki Roshi and

Dainin Katagiri Roshi. She was ordained by Zentatsu Richard Baker in 1977 and received Dharma Transmission from Sojun Mel Weitsman in 1988.

**REVEREND HENG SURE** ordained as a Buddhist *Bhikshu* (monk) at the City of Ten Thousand Buddhas in northern California in 1976. After finishing a master's degree in Oriental languages at the University of California, Berkeley, he received full ordination in the Mahayana tradition of Chinese Buddhism as a disciple of the Venerable Ch'an Master Hsuan Hua. He currently serves as director of the Berkeley Buddhist Monastery and is finishing the doctoral program at the Graduate Theological Union, Berkeley, California.

**VIRGINIA GRAY HENRY** holds degrees from Sarah Lawrence College and Canterbury, Kent. She has published in the field of religion since 1979 and won the 1991 and 1993 Best Produced and Designed Book in Great Britain Award. After living in Cairo, she founded and directed the Islamic Texts Society and Quinta Essentia in Cambridge, England. Back home in Kentucky, she founded and directed Fons Vitae, a company devoted to publishing scholarly interfaith works. She helped found the Thomas Merton Foundation and is on its board and programs committee. Fons Vitae has been publishing a Merton Series in conjunction with the Merton Foundation. It includes: *Merton and Sufism: The Untold Story, Merton and Hesychasm: Prayer of the Heart,* and *Merton and Judaism: Holiness in Words.*

**FATHER KEVIN HUNT, O.C.S.O.,** has been a Trappist monk for forty-nine years. He is a professed monk at St. Joseph's Abbey in Spencer, Massachusetts. Currently he is also a Dharma holder in the White Plum tradition of Japanese Zen.

**STEPHANIE KAZA** is associate professor of environmental studies at the University of Vermont, where she teaches religion and ecology. She is a practitioner of Soto Zen Buddhism and affiliated with Green Gulch Zen Center in California. She is author of *The Attentive Heart: Conversations with Trees* and coeditor of *Dharma Rain: Sources of Buddhist Environmentalism.*

**FATHER THOMAS KEATING, O.C.S.O.,** has been a member of the Cistercian order since 1944. He has been abbot of St. Joseph's Abbey in Spencer, Massachusetts, and superior of St. Benedict's Monastery in Snowmass, Colorado, where he now resides. He is one of the architects of the Centering Prayer movement and of Contemplative Outreach. Active in interreligious dialogue, he founded the Snowmass Interreligious Conference in 1982. His books include *Open Mind, Open Heart; The Mystery of Christ; Invitation to Love; Intimacy with God;* and *The Human Condition.*

**FATHER LEO D. LEFEBURE** is a priest of the Archdiocese of Chicago and an associate professor of theology at Fordham University, New York. He is the editor of *Chicago Studies* and is an editor-at-large for *The Christian Century.* He serves as an advisor to the Monastic Interreligious Dialogue board and is a member of the Faiths in the World Committee of the National Association of Diocesan Ecumenical Officers. He is the author of four books, including *The Buddha and the Christ* and *Revelation, the Religions, and Violence.*

**JOHN DAIDO LOORI** is the abbot and resident teacher at Zen Mountain Monastery in Mt. Tremper, New York. He is founder and director of the Mountains and Rivers Order, an organization of associated Zen Buddhist temples, practice centers, and meditation groups in the United States and abroad. A successor to Maezumi Roshi, he is trained in both *koan* Zen and Dogen's Zen. His books include *The Eight Gates of Zen; Shikantaza: The Art of Just Sitting; Making Love with Light; The Heart of Being: Moral and Ethical Teachings of Zen;* and *Still Point: A Beginner's Guide to Zen Meditation.*

**SISTER KATHY LYZOTTE, O.C.S.O.**, is a Trappistine nun of Our Lady of the Mississippi Abbey in Dubuque, Iowa. She has held administrative positions in her community since 1988 and is a Monastic Interreligious Dialogue board member. A majority of the community at Mississippi Abbey, including Sister Kathy, have received training in dialogue process by Brother Ronald Fogarty, F.M.S., and training in contemplative practice by Sister Ludwigis Fabian, O.S.B.

**FATHER FELIX A. MACHADO** was a Marathi Catholic priest of the Archdiocese of Bombay for twenty-three years and now of Vasai Diocese, Maharashtra, India. He studied in India, France, and the United States, with a doctorate from Fordham University. He was appointed Undersecretary of the

Vatican's Pontifical Council for Interreligious Dialogue by His Holiness Pope John Paul II in 1999. He is visiting lecturer to the Pontifical Urban University and the Pontifical Institute for Educational Sciences, Auxilium, in Rome. He is also author of three books, including *Jnaneshvari Path to Liberation.*

**LAMA ERIC MARCOUX** was a Trappist monk from his thirteenth through his twenty-third year at Gethsemani Abbey and Holy Trinity Abbey. He is a retired psychotherapist as well as a painter and potter, and is active in ecumenical dialogue. He is a disciple of Trungpa Rinpoche and Situ Rinpoche and has been the resident lama of The Waking Peacock Sangha in Portland, Oregon, since 1986.

**SISTER BARBARA McCRACKEN, O.S.B.,** is a Benedictine monastic of Mt. St. Scholastica in Atchison, Kansas. She has been involved in social justice for many years, is a faculty member of Donnelly College, and has also lived and worked with the homeless. Currently she serves the Archdiocese of Kansas City, Kansas, in the Department of Parish Ministries as a consultant for peace and justice.

**PRIORESS MARGARET MICHAUD, O.S.B.,** is a member of the Monastic Interreligious Dialogue board and is prioress of Saint Bede Monastery in Eau Claire, Wisconsin. From 1981 to 1991 she was president of the Federation of Saint Benedict, an association of thirteen monasteries of Benedictine women with houses in the United States, Japan, Taiwan, the Bahamas, and Puerto Rico.

**DONALD W. MITCHELL** is professor of philosophy and chair of religious studies at Purdue University. He is a member of the Focolare Movement and an advisor on dialogue for Monastic Interreligious Dialogue, the Vatican's Pontifical Council for Interreligious Dialogue, and the United States Conference of Catholic Bishops. He is also coordinator of the International Buddhist-Christian Theological Encounter and a founding member of the Society for Buddhist-Christian Studies. Among his publications are *Spirituality and Emptiness; Masao Abe: A Zen Life of Dialogue;* and *Buddhism: Introducing the Buddhist Experience.* He is also coeditor of *The Gethsemani Encounter* and the present work.

**REVEREND SHOHAKU OKUMURA** is a Soto Zen priest and Dharma successor of Kosho Uchiyama Roshi. He has practiced at Antaiji and Zuioji in Japan and has taught at Kyoto Soto Zen Center and Minnesota Zen Meditation Center. Currently he is the head teacher of Sanshin Zen Community in Bloomington, Indiana, and has been the director of Soto Zen Education Center of North America in San Francisco since 1997. He has been working on translation of Dogen's and Uchiyama Roshi's writings. Several of his translations have been published, including *Dogen's Pure Standard for Zen Community: A Translation of* Eihei Shingi*; Shobogenzo Zuimonki: Sayings of Eihei Dogen Zenji; Dogen Zen; Opening the Hand of*

*Thought;* and *Zen Teaching of* Homeless *Kodo.* He is a coeditor of *Nothing Is Hidden* and the editor of *Sitting Under the Bodhi Tree: Lectures on Dogen Zenji's* Bendowa.

**KATE OLSON** is a program officer at the Fetzer Institute. For seventeen years she worked for PBS's flagship news program, *The NewsHour with Jim Lehrer,* specializing in religion coverage. She attended the first Gethsemani Encounter and produced a segment on the event for the *NewsHour.*

**VENERABLE CHUEN PHANGCHAM** is a teacher at the Midwest Buddhist Meditation Center in Warren, Michigan. He is also an insight meditation teacher at Wat Dhammaram in Chicago. He is an official on the Council of Thai *Bhikkus* in the United States and has been president of the Buddhist Council of the Midwest and copresident of the American Buddhist Congress.

**BROTHER PAUL QUENON, O.C.S.O.,** has been a monk of Gethsemani Abbey for forty-three years. From West Virginia, he had his novitiate formation under Thomas Merton. He is a poet, a photographer, and an instructor for monks in formation. He is also on the board of directors for the Thomas Merton Foundation and for the International Thomas Merton Society.

**FATHER THOMAS RYAN, C.S.P.,** directs the Paulist North American Office for Ecumenical and Interfaith Relations in New York City. Previously he served for fourteen years as director of the Canadian Centre for Ecumenism in Montreal and for five years as director of Unitas, an ecumenical center for spirituality and Christian meditation in Montreal. He leads retreats in North America and Europe and has authored several books on the spiritual life, including *Prayer of the Heart and Body.*

**SAMU SUNIM** is the president of the Buddhist Society for Compassionate Wisdom, a North American Buddhist Order, and the publisher of a quarterly Buddhist magazine, *Spring Wind: Buddhist Cultural Forum.* He is the Zen Master of Zen Buddhist Temple, with sites in Chicago, Ann Arbor, and Toronto.

**JUDITH SIMMER-BROWN** has practiced Tibetan Buddhism for thirty years and is an *acharya* (senior Dharma teacher) of the Shambhala Buddhist lineage. She is professor of religious studies at Naropa University in Boulder, Colorado, and has been involved in international Buddhist-Christian dialogue for the past twenty years. Her books include *Dakini's Warm Breath: The Feminine Principle in Tibetan Buddhism,* and she was a contributor to *Benedict's Dharma.*

**FATHER WILLIAM SKUDLAREK, O.S.B.,** the president of Monastic Interreligious Dialogue, has been a monk of Saint John's Abbey, Collegeville, Minnesota, since 1958 and a priest since 1964. He has a doctorate in homiletics from Princeton Theological Seminary. In addition to twenty years on the theology faculty of Saint John's University and

Seminary, he did missionary work in Brazil and Japan. He studied *zazen* at the San'un Zendo in Kamakura, Japan. Currently he serves as administrative assistant to the abbot of Saint John's Abbey.

GESHE LHUNDUB SOPA was born in 1923 in Tibet. Ordained a novice monk at the age of nine, he entered the famed Gaden Chokor Monastery. In 1941, at the age of eighteen, he was admitted to the Tsangpa House of Sery Jey Monastery. He was chosen as one of His Holiness the Dalai Lama's debate examiners in 1959. In 1962 His Holiness the Dalai Lama appointed him tutor to three young recognized incarnate monks, and the four of them moved to the Lamaist Buddhist Monastery in New Jersey. In 1967 he joined the faculty of the University of Wisconsin. He recently retired and now directs the Deer Park Buddhist Center in Wisconsin, which he founded in 1979.

FATHER COLUMBA STEWART, O.S.B., professed vows in 1982 as a monk of Saint John's Abbey in Collegeville, Minnesota. He serves as the monastery's director of formation and teaches monastic studies in the Graduate School of Theology of Saint John's University. He has published extensively in early Christian monastic history and spirituality and is the author of *Cassian the Monk* and *Prayer and Community*.

AJAHN SUNDARA, born in France, was one of the first four women ordained in England by Ajahn Sumedho in 1979 in the Thai Forest Tradition of Ajahn Chah. Since then she has been involved in the establishment and the training of the nuns' community at Chithurst and Amaravati Buddhist Monasteries in England. In the mid-1990s she spent over two years in Thailand practicing in forest monasteries. She teaches and leads meditation retreats in Europe and the United States and is interested in exploring ways of practicing, sustaining, and integrating Buddhist teachings in Western culture. She is currently living at Abhayagiri Monastery in California.

**GESHE LOBSANG TENZIN** was born in Kinnaur, a small Himalayan kingdom adjoining Tibet. At the age of fourteen he received his ordination from His Holiness the Dalai Lama and began training at the Buddhist School of Dialectics, the private school of His Holiness in Dharamsala, India. In 1985 he entered the Drepung Loseling Monastic College in southern India to continue his training. In 1991 he was sent to Atlanta by the monastery to establish and oversee Drepung Loseling Institute. In 1994 he was awarded the degree of Geshe Lharampa from Drepung Loseling Monastery. In 1999 he received his Ph.D. from Emory University, where he now teaches.

**FATHER DAMIEN THOMPSON, O.C.S.O.**, is abbot of Gethsemani Abbey. He entered the monastery in 1978, after being a member of Maryknoll.

**FATHER JULIAN VON DUERBECK, O.S.B.**, is a monk of St. Procopius Abbey and adjunct professor of the history of religions at Benedictine University in Lisle, Illinois. He has served on the board of Monastic Interreligious Dialogue and assisted in the planning of both Gethsemani Encounters. He is also a member of the International Chivalric Institute and is a knight of the Noble Company of the Rose.

**FATHER DANIEL J. WARD, O.S.B.**, is a monk of St. John's Abbey in Collegeville, Minnesota. He is on the Monastic Interreligious Dialogue board and is the executive director of Legal Resource Center for Religious in Silver Spring, Maryland. He was formerly professor of canon and civil law at St. John's University, where he founded the Monastic Institute.

**FATHER JAMES WISEMAN, O.S.B.**, is a monk of St. Anselm's Abbey in Washington, D.C., where he currently is serving as prior of the monastic community. He is an associate professor and chair of the Department of Theology at The Catholic University of America. He was chair of Monastic Interreligious Dialogue from 1994 to 1999 and has been editor of the *MID Bulletin* since 1998. He was coeditor of *The Gethsemani Encounter* and coeditor of the present work. His other books include *Light from Light: An Anthology of Christian Mysticism* and *Theology and Modern Science: Quest for Coherence.*

**KAROL WOJTYLA, HIS HOLINESS POPE JOHN PAUL II**, has been the spiritual leader of the Roman Catholic Church since his election as pope in 1978. Born in Wadowice, Poland, in 1920, he is the most widely traveled and one of the longest reigning popes in the history of the church, and is widely credited with having given the Polish people the courage to resist and eventually overcome Communist rule. Pope John Paul has also been very active in promoting interreligious dialogue. His major encyclicals include *Sollicitudo Rei Socialis* (1987), *Veritatis Splendor* (1993), and *Evangelium Vitae* (1995).

**FATHER JOSEPH WONG, O.S.B. CAM.**, originally from Hong Kong, is a monk of New Camaldoli Hermitage in Big Sur, California, and director of junior monks. He completed his doctorate in theology at the Gregorian University in Rome, and taught systematic theology and spirituality in Rome and at Sheshan Seminary in Shanghai, China. He is a Monastic Interreligious Dialogue board member and chairman of the Camaldolese Institute for East-West Dialogue in Big Sur. He is the author of many articles as well as the coeditor of *Purity of Heart and Contemplation: A Monastic Dialogue Between Christian and Asian Traditions*.

# Index

Tibet and Tibetan Buddhism:
Buddhism, concept of taking and
giving, 17–18, 19, 203;
Buddhism, verse, 19; Buddhism,
"view and action," 142–43; love,
types of in, 70–71; nuns, 174;
stories of oppression, torture,
exile, xi, 44–45
Tozan, Master, 220
transcendence of suffering, 10
transformation: experiences of
personal, 47; of negative karma,
19; of others, by unity, 20–21; of
self, through taking and giving,
19; through sickness and aging,
189–90, 199–201; through
suffering, xiv, 11, 13–14, 15, 24,
40, 51, 65, 189, 199–201
Trappist monks, 108; killed in North
Africa, xi, 241; monastic life, 40
Trungpa Rinpoche, 45–46

University of Peace, Costa Rica,
156
unworthiness, 90–104. *See also*
emotions, afflictive

veil of Veronica, 48–49
violence, 2, 141–82; Abhidharma
tradition, five factors of, 142;
attachment to views and, 157–58;
blaming and, 149–50; breaking
the cycle, Jesus example, 152–53,
155; Buddhism, pacifism and,
155, 156–57; Conception Abbey,
shootings at, 241–43; Dalai Lama
on, 142, 143, 160; education of
children and, 145–46; facing
limitations and, 150–53;

forgiveness and redemptive
suffering, 242–43; hatred and,
142, 143, 149, 153–54, 239–40;
inner, 150; institutional power
and, 165–67, 168–70; long-term
approach, 158–59, 161;
mindfulness and, 148; organizing
for decency, 146–47; patriarchy
and, 165–66; pervasiveness of,
161–64; religious, 87, 157–58;
sexual abuse, 175–79; structures
of peace and, 156; technology
and, 160; types of, 161–64; "view
and action," 142–43. *See also*
terrorism
von Duerbeck, Father Julian,
197–98, 211–12, 259–60
vulnerability, 108–9

Ward, Father Daniel, 38–39, 132,
164–66, 176–77, 260
*When a Pope Asks Forgiveness*, 103
Wiseman, Father James, x, 77–78,
95–98, 103, 123–24, 139–40,
222, 260
Wong, Father Joseph, 48–49,
61–62, 154, 199–201, 215,
224–25, 261
world, humans as stewards of,
78–79

Zen: death, view of, 228; *koans*, 12,
14, 92; life after death and, 226;
liturgies, 12–13; monastic life,
11–12; nondualistic mind, 162;
precepts, 12, 157; Soto, 14;
teaching stories, 92; *zazen* (sitting
meditation), 12, 91–92, 106
*Zorba the Greek* (film), 100

—